Kundalini E   Awakening

A Spiritual Guide for Beginners to Activate
Your Mind's Psychic Intuition and Power,
Raise your Vibration with Yoga for
Transcendence and Enlightenment

Melissa Gomes

https://smartpa.ge/MelissaGomes

Table of Contents

FREEBIES

AND

RELATED PRODUCTS

WORKBOOKS
AUDIOBOOKS
FREE BOOKS
REVIEW COPIES

HERE

HTTPS://SMARTPA.GE/MELISSAGOMES

Freebies!

I have a **special treat for you**! You can access exclusive bonuses I created specifically for my readers at the following link! The link will redirect you to a webpage containing all my books and bonuses for each book. Just select the book you have purchased and check the bonuses!

>> https://smartpa.ge/MelissaGomes<<

OR scan the QR Code with your phone's camera

Bonus 1: Free Workbook - Value 12.95$

This **workbook** will guide you with **specific questions** and give you all the space you need to write down the answers. Taking time for **self-reflection** is extremely valuable, especially when looking to develop new skills and **learn** new concepts. I highly suggest you *grab this complimentary workbook for yourself*, as it will help you gain clarity on your goals. Some authors like to sell the workbook, but I think giving it away for free is the perfect way to say **"thank you" to my readers**.

Bonus 2: Free Book - Value 12.95$

Grab a **free short book** with **22+ Techniques for Meditation**. The book will introduce you to a range of meditation practices you can use to help you develop your inner awareness, inner calm, and overall sense of well-being. You will also learn how to begin a meditation practice that works for you regardless of your schedule. These meditation techniques work for everyone, regardless of age or fitness level. Check it out at the link below!

Bonus 3: Free audiobook - Value 14.95$

If you love listening to audiobooks on the go or would enjoy a narration as you read along, I have great news for you. You can download the audiobook version of *my books* for **FREE** just by signing up for a FREE 30-day Audible trial! You can find the audio versions of my books (depending on availability) at the following link.

Join my Review Team!

Are you an avid reader looking to have more insights into spirituality? Do you want to get free books in exchange for an honest review? You can do so by joining my Review Team! You will get priority access to my books before they are released. You only need to follow me on Booksprout, and you will get notified every time a new Review Copy is available for my latest release!

For all the Freebies, visit the following link:

>> https://smartpa.ge/MelissaGomes<<

OR scan the QR Code with your phone's camera.

I'm here because of you

When you're supporting an independent author,
you're supporting a dream. Please leave an honest review on Amazon by scanning the QR code below and clicking on the "Leave an Amazon Review" Button.

★★★★★

https://smartpa.ge/MelissaGomes

Chapter 1: What Exactly is Kundalini?

Kundalini is an image created by the ancient Indians to express their feelings about divinity. Kundalini is also concerned with healing on all levels, and you can use it to reverse maladaptive processes and initiate deeper, long-lasting healing. It is a deep and dynamic force situated at the base of your spine, and it is here that all our spiritual and physical life-force energy originates.

The spiral of our energy sings from its core outward; this energy, when awakened healthily, reaches into the cells of our body and energies, healing and rejuvenating them. When the cells are allowed to become imbalanced energetically, they can begin to malfunction and become "stuck," where they then begin to cause you harm and discomfort.

Kundalini is the physical manifestation of a very deep unconscious force attached and anchored deep in the cells of our physical being; the forces of life and consciousness connect you to your Higher Self. This extraordinary force has always been there and lies dormant until needed in times of stress or crisis. Once this primal energy is aroused and activated, it influences you on a very deep and basic energy level.

Kundalini can only awaken after we awaken first. It first requires our conscious intent and, if we can, our willingness to consciously create our unique healing experience. This may sound lofty or complicated, but it becomes very simple and straightforward once you feel secure enough in your practice to allow the vital energies of your being to operate freely and undisturbed.

To experience this natural energetic healing, we must pose the question of why it is that we need to heal in the first place. Usually, when we begin working on our healing experiences, we will discover that we need our energy to flow healthily and that doing things in different ways yields different results for us. Kundalini healing works on energetic and foundational levels simultaneously. It corrects imbalances of raw energy by shifting deep-held triggers of fear and trauma stored in the cells. Once the body has been cleared of these blocks, it can move on to experience new and creative states of awareness.

Your Kundalini healing experience is one that you can actively participate in and commit to. The imbalances corrected during the healing process are still your responsibility. When imbalances are produced, and the body's energies begin to process them for you, they give messages that need to be addressed to move forward productively. This effect is why it is important to participate fully in your healing. Your health will bring you many gifts, including love for yourself and others, the ability to let go, and greater wisdom about how life works.

Before we get into the specifics of Kundalini and its awakening, we must understand the terms Kundalini and chakras in the next chapter. This can help you better prepare for the process and realize the power you can activate using your Kundalini.

History of Awakening

Around 3,000 BC, ancient Indians began speaking and writing about Kundalini, which they believed was the link to the universe's sacred and divine energy. They believed that Kundalini was the very breath of life itself. Kundalini usually has translated as "coiled" or "bound". The Sanskrit word for energy or spirit is "prana", which means "breath". So the Sanskrit word for Kundalini is "the coiled or bound prana of the spiritual world- the cosmic breath of life, the dynamic power that lies at the wellhead of universal consciousness." The Hindus believed that a person's flow or production of kundalini depended on the quality of their consciousness.

Kundalini existed in ancient Egypt and ancient India. The ankh symbol, which represents the union of masculine and feminine energy, was used as a spiritual talisman and a symbol of alignment with source potential. Kundalini is found in many ancient cultures, but as a universal phenomenon, it is only very recently that it has taken root in the present-day West. In Hindu tradition, the pituitary and pineal brains were believed to be the caves of kundalini. In India, it is believed that the brain receives complete and direct access to the soul through the pineal gland, which is why Kundalini is considered the key to awakening the soul in yoga.

The chakras are seven energy centers located along the body's central channel to the crown of our head. Each chakra is associated with a specific color that helps stimulate them. It has also been suggested that each chakra symbology has a corresponding sound that can help stimulate their activation. When the chakras are stimulated, their energy centers become active to resuscitate your Kundalini energy. This takes place when the chakras are opened or activated. Kundalini energy is usually dormant in the human system because it needs to be aroused first to rise upward from the root chakra at the base of the spine. Through yoga and other practices, this rejuvenating energy is gradually awakened.

The ancient Chinese believed that chi was the life force energy that existed within us and that returning orgasm energy to the brain could extend the life and reverse the effects of aging. The Tao Te Ching and the I Ching also describe the connection between the body's energy centers and the soul's. The Eastern world uses acupuncture to stimulate and manipulate energy flow through the body's meridian system to sustain a healthy flow of life force energy. It is believed that acupuncture's influence causes the body's energy to circulate through the different energy channels, releasing blockages and toxins and accelerating healing. The Taoists believed that the life force energy surrounding and permeating the cosmos also exists within each person's body.

Kundalini first appears in history with the practice of alchemy. It is an intriguing topic because the more you learn about it, the more you will realize that it overlaps with Kundalini appreciation in Indian tradition and that yoga practice in ancient India also supported kundalini awareness. It is the vital energy that flows through the chakras. You can gain many benefits by awakening the kundalini, including reaching higher planes of consciousness and unlocking your psychic abilities. As awakening the flow of energy in our bodies assists us in becoming transcendent in various ways, it can help us gain insight during difficult times, feel less alone, and find our way in life.

Finally, Kundalini is about healing on all levels. It can be awakened and guided by using meditation methods. In this way, your consciousness takes charge of the channels and can release blockages that don't serve your best interests. As your awareness becomes deeper and more expansive, you can learn to reclaim control over your energy, allowing your fate to be driven by your imagination rather than your fears. The result is a higher state of consciousness and a larger sense of the Self, which helps you master your external environment. The increased psychic ability development creates a heightened awareness of your body's energies and a deepening understanding of your life and spiritual experiences.

Kundalini awareness and awakening have been linked with healing attempts throughout history. Many philosophers, therapists, yogis, and Eastern healing masters have written about kundalini and their work to awaken it. Unfortunately, most of these texts have been lost, so we must rely on their written description and later tradition concerning the actual practices used to awaken kundalini. The following chapters will cover the practices of yoga, tantra yoga, and breathing exercises that help stimulate the chakras and awaken kundalini energy.

There are many creative ways you can support your awakening. You can perform affirmations and visualizations that stimulate your chakras and the chakras of your trusted spiritual guides. You can call on your higher self for guidance during your meditation sessions. Visualizing and listening to music can also trigger your kundalini.

Awakening kundalini energy will lead you on your path to spiritual development. It is a multidimensional process that takes you through many realms, including past-life experiences, ascension energy, and cosmic awareness. As you receive more consciousness and your spiritual awakening, you merge with higher beings, animals, plants, and elemental spirits. Your mind and spirit merge with your soul, and your body's cells create a magnificent Here, you will learn about the energy channels in the physical body and your subtle body.

After understanding more about kundalini, we will examine the main chakras and their associated sounds. Kundalini energy is considered one of the great secrets of spirituality and discovery. Kundalini awakening is the natural flow of life-force energy that exists within us. It is a kundalini yoga technique that stretches and strengthens the spine, alleviates stress, strengthens the nervous system, and stretches the energy channels. The yang practice begins with the asana practice, which loosens the spine and awakens the muscles to full extension. For example, standing postures lengthen the spinal muscles and strengthen the legs and ankles. Also, standing postures lengthen the spinal muscles and strengthen the legs, ankles, knees, and back.

There is no true definition of Kundalini energy because its definition is fluid. It is one of the "worlds within us" and the life force in the universe. Because of its nature, Kundalini's energy cannot be controlled with physical or mental declarations or manipulation. People attempting to harness Kundalini energy usually align with their higher consciousness to access it; however, most people have little experience with kundalini energy beyond the physical senses, so they attempt it prematurely and risk their lives. Of course, people awakened to Kundalini energy have a special awareness and gifts that can assist others.

You can become empowered by uniting your divine Self with your human Self. As you welcome the Kundalini energy into your higher consciousness, your own awakening becomes your companion as you take control of your destiny by working on yourself for the benefit of others. These gifts are rooted in your innate spiritual wisdom and will radiate out, healing those you care about. Gifts of Kundalini, when awakened, include lifting or levitating objects, healing with their hands, reading another person's thoughts, and healing with the power of thought.

Many cults attempt to manipulate kundalini energy and force it to react due to the force of belief. However, this is dangerous and has no lasting benefits. The goal of taking this approach is to compel energy forcefully. The resulting power is usually short-lived because the energy is stirred up and must be forcibly contained. This creates an imbalance in the chakras and can become dangerous.

From a scientific perspective, the chakras are not physical or material. They each manifest as a vortex of psychic energies and energy centers, which receive external input from our physical and subtle bodies. Although a chakra is considered a vortex of energy, its center is also a vortex of psychic energies that pulsate with life force energy. These energies serve as a communication medium between the spiritual and physical worlds.

Pineal Gland Symbolism

The pineal gland, also known as the Third Eye, is the gatekeeper to the spiritual world. It is closely linked with the metaphysical or subtle body, which also houses the soul. The pineal gland contains a small blue light-sensitive pineal body that regulates our body's circadian rhythms or internal timetable. It is a hunter-gatherer of serotonin trips in our brain and body. It is associated with various cognitive centers in the brain and acts as an antenna for electromagnetic frequencies. It also secretes melatonin and prolactin, which regulate our sleep patterns.

The pineal gland institutes the endocrine system's first synthesis process before birth and is involved in our ability to learn. It acts as a bridge between our feet and our heads. It is related to the energy of our spine and is a bridge to the realm of the soul. This bridge is very sensitive and can cause a magnetic field that modifies, regulates, and guides our physical brain, producing psychic phenomena such as vibrations, out-of-body experiences, and hallucinations.

Throughout history, the pinecone has been found to be a symbol of the pineal gland in different cultures. The pinecone is a wisdom sign. The ancients believed that the Goddess of oneness and transformation stands guardian over the worlds, connecting the earth to the celestial spheres, a conduit of our consciousness to awareness and beyond. In Christianity, the pinecone symbolizes enlightenment and rebirth because it rises from its seed. When you meditate, focus on stimulating the pineal gland. You can stimulate it by focusing your mind on the area between your eyes above your eyebrows. You can also place your palm on your third eye during meditation. Focusing on this area can revitalize your energy centers and make you feel more spiritually uplifted.

Manifestation of Psychic Gifts

Gaining psychic gifts is common upon spiritual awakening. Most people are attracted to spirituality because they need to help others and the world around them. These individuals have a natural gift of communicating with people and are aware of universal truths around them. Although your psychic gifts are natural, you can enhance them through meditation and yoga.

Your psychic abilities will either remain dormant or slowly develop as you grow spiritually. If you practice daily meditation, your psychic gifts will most likely reawaken and develop more rapidly. Once you awaken to your inner workings, you will notice when certain people are trying to contact you. You will naturally become sensitive and aware of different energies in your environment and sense someone's presence without consciously visualizing them being there. You may also experience spontaneous revelations, déjà vu, and flashes of inspiration that will alter your perspective toward life or situations. Your intuition will guide you in accomplishing various conscious and unconscious goals. It is through intuitive reading, telepathy, and psychic dream interpretation that you can discern a person's thoughts or actions. Psychic dreams can help reveal events at present or at another timeline in history. These psychic adventures occur for a reason. They are moments that will not be forgotten and may your life's path for the better.

Chapter 2: Chakras and Kundalini

Kundalini is serpent energy that rises and deals with inner movement, healing, and divinity. It is related to the chakras, which drive our body's life force energy. The chakras connect us to the earth and the divine energy of the universe and act as outlets for our energy. When in balance, the chakras help us know ourselves and the world around us; they are healthy conduits for energy to flow. When they are not, we experience poor health, a lack of joy, and a sense of disconnection from the universe.

Each chakra corresponds to a specific body part and balances your entire being. This chakra rules our survival instincts and is about our connection with the planet and other people. When out of balance, we feel a lack or dysfunction in our physical and mental bodies. Consider your body to have seven energetic centers linked to seven glands. When you're ready to embark on a spiritual journey, you'll realize that these blockages and flow-stoppers are embodied in your chakras.

Root Chakra

The first chakra, represented by the red color and named Muladhara in Sanskrit, is an essential chakra for awakening the Kundalini energy the in the base of your spine, where the root chakra is located. The root chakra is associated with the adrenal glands, which act as a sympathetic endocrine gland that regulates your stress level. Because of this, you can also recognize when the root chakra becomes closed or overactive by working with your adrenal glands. Here are ways to check if your root chakra is balanced or not:

- With an open root chakra, energy flow is balanced and easy. You'll experience a sense of security and abundance in your life. You'll be able to accept and receive kindness more easily. Your skin will be radiant and healthy. You enjoy harmony with your body. You will balance your body weight. You'll be able to fall and stay asleep easily. You'll be able to bounce back from illness easily. You will feel abundance in your life. You'll have a strong sense of bonding with the earth.
- You may experience anxiety and stress with an unbalanced root chakra. Your eating habits may be poor, and you may eat too much when stressed - perhaps a comfort-food addiction. You may experience emotional eating to deal with your emotions while feeling powerless - a disempowered "comfort" food. When your adrenal glands are over-activated, and you have little heat in your body, it can cause adrenal fatigue or rigidity. Balance this energy, and you can feel freer from emotional and physical burdens or patterns.

Sacral Chakra

The second chakra, also called Svadhishthana in Sanskrit, is located in your sacrum area and is related to the color orange. It is concerned with creativity, originality, community, trust, pleasure, and movement. It influences your energies of sexuality, reproductive capability, creativity, emotions, pleasure, fertility, lower abdominal, and backside. The sacral plexus chakra is closely connected to the bladder and works as an intermediary between your lower and higher emotional centers.

- A balanced sacral chakra helps you connect deeply with other people. You can feel enriched through your relationships. You can connect through touch. You'll have a comfortable body and enjoy movement. You'll feel great with sexuality. At this level, you can feel that you have a purpose in life. You'll experience a sense of activism, such as standing up for your beliefs. You will start to feel a sense of passion and joy.
- Blockages or reversals of the sacral chakra may manifest as low energy, constant fear, feeling disconnected from the world, eating disorders, overt materialism, difficulty saving money, or general health problems. If this chakra's energy is not flowing properly, your career may stagnate because your creative juices may be clogged. Excessive sexuality can be a sign of blocked sacral chakra energy. You may fear the loss of intimacy and connection in life and have become so afraid of intimacy that you have completely disconnected from it. You may experience anger and frustration about these feelings if your sacral chakra is left unchecked.

Solar Plexus Chakra

The third chakra is situated at the center of the upper stomach area, related to the color yellow. It is known as Manipura in Sanskrit, which deals with willpower and self-esteem. It also treats digestive issues, anxiety, self-esteem, and the body's detoxification system. It is where your energies of confidence will flourish when you open this chakra.

- Suppose your solar plexus chakra is balanced and aligned. In that case, your life force energy, the kundalini, can freely flow, enabling you to make decisions based on your intuition and inner guidance system. As this chakra restores the balance of yin and yang energies in your body, it allows you to be content within yourself while appreciating the world around you.

- When your third chakra is blocked, you can experience anxiety, tension, depression, and anger. You may have difficulty making decisions or managing challenges in your life. You have low self-confidence and low self-esteem. You may experience depression in relationships with others and be unable to express your emotions easily. You may be a perfectionist and have difficulties letting go. You might also experience unexplained pain in your upper stomach area or abdomen, acidic feelings in your stomach, difficulty expressing yourself, and poor digestion, leading to panic attacks or depression.

Heart Chakra

The fourth chakra is located in the chest area, colored green, and is called Anahata in Sanskrit. It represents love, forgiveness, compassion, joy, and gratitude. It is concerned with selflessness and family or partnership. The heart chakra can help awaken your Kundalini in your spine by balancing how you emotionally handle situations and events in your life.

- A balanced heart chakra helps you feel calm and relaxed. You tend to be more joyful, loving, and balanced if these energies are aligned. Connecting to your fourth chakra helps you feel your feelings deeply so you can also forgive and let go of any past traumas and help you experience more compassion.
- An unbalanced heart chakra can create fear, anxiety, and anger. You should feel emotional freedom to express love, compassion, joy, and gratitude. You shouldn't be afraid of expressing your true feelings. A blocked heart chakra can also lead to physical symptoms like ulcers, heartburn, and digestive issues.

Throat Chakra

The Vishuddha, or fifth chakra, is located in the middle of your throat and is related to your thyroid and the color blue. It deals with communication, self-expression, creativity, learning, and ego. Your throat chakra influences your ability to handle stress and your voice and sound production abilities. The throat chakra also governs the thyroid gland and regulates your digestion system.

- When your throat chakra is open, you can express yourself freely. An open throat chakra also helps you speak your truth. You can sing or speak in public more easily. You will experience a sense of anticipation when you await your words, and you'll be able to express yourself romantically. You'll love listening to the sound of your voice and might enjoy singing. You'll be able to speak freely and truthfully to others. Your voice, communication abilities, and self-expression become open to the world.
- When your throat chakra is imbalanced, Manifestations are often blocked and can produce voice issues. You have difficulty speaking and expressing yourself. Oversharing, sore throats, asthma, anemia, constant fatigue, or conflict avoidance are all symptoms of throat chakra blockages. If your throat chakra is blocked, you won't be able to speak your truth or voice your opinions freely. Your voice may become hoarse and disconnected from your inner self.

Third Eye Chakra

The sixth chakra is in the center of the forehead and is colored indigo. It is called Ajna and governs your intuition, wisdom, hallucinations, and out-of-body experiences. The sixth chakra

23

governs your intuition and connection to the spiritual world and is also connected with wisdom and creativity. You can see the future or past from your sixth chakra or imagine any experience you'd like to have.

- When your third eye chakra is balanced, you gain many benefits, including healing, strength, and inspiration. You can connect with your spirit guides and dreams more easily at this stage of spiritual awakening. You'll have a better understanding of your life's path. You'll feel a sense of fearlessness and develop strong mental and spiritual energy that helps you connect with your unconscious mind.
- When your sixth chakra is blocked, you might experience depression, a lack of direction in life or wisdom, and spiritual confusion. Perhaps you feel obstructed in your search for inner peace or enlightenment. You might feel blocked mentally or spiritually in some way. You may feel confused or overwhelmed by the mind's chatter, unable to resolve the confusion in your mind. It might also manifest physical symptoms like migraines, insomnia, eye or vision problems, depression, high blood pressure, inability to recall one's dreams, schizophrenia, and paranoia, which can, later on, become a history of mental disorders.

Crown Chakra

The seventh chakra is at the top of the head and is called the Sahasrara in Sanskrit. It improves psychic abilities, spirituality, connection with divinity, a sense of purpose and mission, life direction, and awareness of cosmic reality. It represents your divine connection to Source with a high sense of spirituality and overall enlightenment. These higher energies around your crown chakra provide you with enhanced chakra activation and a higher journey of consciousness.

- When your crown chakra is opened, you will have more inner peace and inner bliss. Connecting to your crown chakra will help you achieve a higher sense of intuition and knowledge. You may even experience guided visions and astral projection, along with gaining psychic gifts like telepathy, clairaudience, or clairvoyance.
- Blockages in the crown chakra may manifest as feelings of greed, intense depression, the need for dominance over others, self-destructive behaviors, or generally destructive behaviors. When your crown chakra is blocked, you may experience physical disorders like anxiety, fear, stress, spiritual confusion, or spiritual addiction. You may also experience insomnia or migraine headaches. If you suffer from migraines, they may manifest as physical tension or contractions in your head and neck. Other physical symptoms may include cold hands and feet, fatigue, low blood pressure, irregular heartbeats or rapid breathing, muscular aches or cramping in the neck and shoulders, and pain behind your eyes.

When all your chakras are balanced and aligned, your body will operate at its optimal level, and you can experience a balanced life. When just one chakra is unbalanced or blocked, this can lead to a physical or emotional imbalance that can manifest as an illness. Every physical or emotional problem begins in your mind and manifests in the body. Balance your chakras by choosing the following methods: meditation, goddess worship, yoga, acupuncture, chanting mantras, repeating positive affirmations, singing, dancing, or attending spiritual retreats.

You may not be aware that you can unlock these chakras and awaken your kundalini energies with the practice of yoga or meditation techniques. Connecting your chakras may help you to combat physical and emotional ailments and achieve spiritual enlightenment. Your chakras affect every part of your body and psyche, yet they are hidden from most. There are ways to open them that can provide you with the health and peace of mind you desire. You may linger in spiritual and alignment blocks until you realize that you need assistance to move these blockages.

Chakras generally teach you about your emotions, how you live your reality, and how to manage your life. Chakras are normally separated into seven groups that affect our whole body. While each chakra represents a specific element and power center in your body, you may also experience blockages or reversals. You may become stuck in unhealthy thoughts, patterns, and emotions when blockages occur. Your chakras store our energetic and physical energies as energy at the time of conception. Your chakras are connected with important glands in your brain that manage your hormonal impulses. During puberty, your chakras become activated, especially your energy centers related to your sex organs. Your chakras may close because of the stress from childbirth or as a protective mechanism.

There are ways to balance your chakras and achieve a healthier balance in your emotions, physical health, and spirituality. Balancing the chakras may help energize your mind, body, and spirit. You can balance your chakras with meditation, chanting mantras, yoga, or goddess worship. Meditation can realign your chakras, transform negative energies, and clear out any emotional blockages that may have formed. You may restore healthy energy flows with Reiki and other forms of energy healing. Spiritual guides can also help you restore these balances and address any problems by consulting with them during meditation as you ascend to your Higher Self.

Chapter 3: What Should You Do with Your Kundalini?

You can use the kundalini to align and open the chakras even more than you could once blockages and energetic reversals have been cleared. The different chakra colors relate to the meridians of the vital organs in the body. A block in any chakra shows up in a different area of your body, just like the color can give a sense or feeling of the corresponding chakra.

You can also use Kundalini for various other purposes, such as interacting between the chakras and balancing multiple chakras at once. Below you will find some of the most effective methods of achieving Kundalini activation.

The best and most popular method for taking to Kundalini is meditation. This has been done for ages, but we now live in a time of instant gratification. Most people don't have the time to just sit in one place and meditate when they could do something more active like climbing, running, swimming, or cycling to achieve the same result. However, meditation will greatly enhance the energies of everything you do.

What is unique about meditation is that you don't have actually to sit and breathe a certain way. Instead, you can meditate through music, movement, and visualization. You can begin by meditating on shakti and prana to become more aware of your kundalini, which will help you become more aware of your body, others, and the world. Then, you can visualize activating your chakras, either the different colors or the spinning discs of light, as well as visualizing the flow of kundalini energy going up through the chakras. This will help you get in the meditation mood easily and quickly, and always remember to open your chakras before beginning the practice of Kundalini Yoga.

Another very effective way to experience Kundalini is practicing pranayama and breathing exercises. Practicing pranayama will help you to learn how to control your breath and create an awareness that will assist in kundalini awakening through directed breath and body movements. Again, this is ideal for those who don't like sitting still to meditate but still want to experience the heightened awareness that meditation provides.

When you practice breathing exercises, you can focus on different points in your body that will aid in opening the chakras and awakening your kundalini. Meridian lines connect these points to the different chakras. By focusing your breath on a particular body area while moving your hands over the same area, you can heighten your awareness of the corresponding chakra and activate it. You can also focus on a mantra while doing the asanas and movements.

Kundalini yoga is another method that aids in the activation of your kundalini. The techniques and poses used in yoga will also help open your chakras and your body even further. Kundalini yoga will also help you focus your energy to control it better, which is one of the most important factors for those wanting to activate their kundalini.

Kundalini yoga is like other types of yoga, focusing on meditation, asana, and breathing. You can begin and move through the traditional Kundalini yoga and practice Kundalini Yoga Nidra, which is extremely relaxing and refreshing. We all want to have more control over our lives. By using the methods of activating your kundalini, you will not only feel more alive than ever, but you will also experience one hundred percent clarity, happiness, and enlightenment.

Kundalini awakening will assist you in connecting with your innate psychic abilities. These abilities can assist you with your soul mission. This awakening process can also lead to mystical connection and enlightenment. Your body will begin to heal naturally, and you will notice personality shifts, connections with spirit guides and guardians, the release of old fears, and other changes.

When your kundalini is engaged and active, you will feel more confident, brave, worthy, and inspired to carry out your soul mission. You will also become aware of your intuitive abilities to help yourself and others in your world. Meditation is the best way to begin this process, but you can use methods like kundalini yoga to guide you further and make you more aware and centered. You will also want to help those you care about and serve those you know are in need.

You can direct Kundalini energy toward any goal, whether manifestation, healing, attraction, or anything else. It will allow you to act in ways that attract exactly what you want. One of the most common reasons people try to activate their kundalini is to know how to manifest their desires, especially financial success. You can direct your kundalini energy toward creating anything. Many who have done this method have manifested extremely amazing things, from money to new jobs to happiness at the end of their life. Remember that your kundalini can be used in a constant stream of energy or as a way to direct your will toward the things you wish to manifest. You can create daily rituals to help manifest your goals and desires, and your kundalini awakening will give you the confidence to live your dream life.

You can also use this method of awakening to help heal yourself and others with your mind, body, and soul. You can use Kundalini energy for healing and transformation in numerous ways. You can direct this energy inward toward healing and transformation within your soul or circulate it outward toward healing others. You can become as effective as you want in helping to heal others.

By awakening your kundalini, you can fertilize your psychic senses to help manifest your dreams and desires. This meditation will help you to connect more deeply with your chakras, awaken your kundalini, activate abilities, and move through your life.

Frequently Asked Questions

This section will briefly overview Kundalini, its benefits, and some proper awakening techniques.

1. **How do you define Kundalini?** Kundalini is a vessel through which shakti energy flows in the human body. It inspires artistic creation and reproductive procreation in the human realm. It controls the ever-changing flow of energy in the human body. It is responsible for the activity which results in endocrine and nervous system functions. It forms an integral part of the nervous system and is considered the most subtle and elusive part of the human organism. The energy lies deep within the Earth's molten core and spirals upward through the entire mountain chain, the axis, up to the earth's surface.
2. **How soon will I feel the effects of Kundalini awakening?** Depending on how one spends their life, it can be immediate, or it may take several weeks or months. If you are intensely working to develop your inner consciousness, you will activate your kundalini within 21 days.
3. **Is there a particular body position someone should adopt while meditating?** Yes, one should sit with the

spine erect and the feet firmly grounded on a firm surface, such as a stable bench or the floor.

4. **Are there any specific foods that can accelerate the activation of Kundalini?** Several foods can enhance Kundalini activation. These include sesame seeds, goji berries, milk, oranges, and raisins.

5. **What is so infectious about Kundalini awakening?** The increased awareness and the resulting supernatural powers exhibited by Kundalini-awakened individuals are infectious because the ability to achieve superhuman abilities is still thought to reside within each individual.

6. **How should I go about increasing the Kundalini energy in the body?** First, it is important to understand that Kundalini doesn't have a location as such - it is a concept. Kundalini is the dormant energy lying dormant deep within you that is responsible for activating all aspects of your life. When you have it ignited within your body, it should rush up your spine resulting in your consciousness being heightened through the window of your third eye. When you awaken the chakras, your kundalini is inevitably awakened.

7. **What three factors can keep an individual from experiencing Kundalini awakening?** The three primary factors are excessive mental chatter, fear, and stress.

8. **What are the three ways in which you can awaken Kundalini?** The three ways to awaken your Kundalini are: through the transmission of energy transmitted to it through another, through meditation, and rigorous sternness while meditating.

9. **What is the primary purpose of the Kundalini?** The primary purpose of the Kundalini is to awaken, energize, and protect the individual's inner consciousness. Kundalini awakens the deep dormant energy in each

individual's core and the spiritual side of an individual's nature.

10. **Does Kundalini unlock one's mind's eye?** Kundalini unlocks one's mind's eye but is determined not to do so until the individual reaches the end of the evolution cycle. However, it becomes a gradual process through which an individual experiences extraordinary changes in their consciousness and begins to awaken their third eye.

11. **Do any of the ritualistic and Tantric practices of Kundalini awakening attract evil spirits?** No, they do not. These are methods to awaken your inner self and bring it to the surface, and this ultimately helps you to become aware of your spiritual side. This, in turn, helps cleanse as well as help you protect your body from other energies that exist in your individual's etheric and astral bodies.

12. **How can I stop my kundalini arousal?** Become aware of the sensations as they appear and remember that your body is merely forced to move and awaken in response to a thousand thoughts. When you see each feeling for what it is, it is easier to move past each feeling and refocus on the task at hand.

Kundalini yoga is directly related to kundalini awakening because it ensures that the body and mind balance. It is a physical and mental practice that helps to release built-up energy from the body through the breath and positioning of the body. It helps unlock the energy stored in the body before you attempt to awaken the kundalini.

How do I help balance my mental and physical energies? The chakras are our body's energy centers, sometimes called "energy wheels," found in our bodies. These openings are where energy enters the body and where it is dispersed. Originally they were thought to have spiritual significance, but in modern science, we know they have nothing in our ego world. The chakras, balancing your energy, help you maintain your health and keep your energy well distributed. This is the benchmark of balancing your body and mind; it is achieved through breath and exercise.

The chakras organize the flow of vital cosmic energy throughout the body and mind. They distribute vital energy to all body parts and organs. Balancing the chakras can occur through exercise, massage, diet, meditation, or bioenergy therapies.

When can one expect the results of the awakening or kundalini experience? The results can manifest instantly. The pinnacle chakra awakens instantly. The experience is a recognition of your connection to the world around you.

Kundalini awakening is a process that includes meditation, yoga, introspection, self-and-world analysis, and other practices. You'll find yourself buzzing, having more synchronicities, and being guided to work through old emotional and physical wounds.

Going Through the Awakening Process

Things may be dramatic and painful at the start of your kundalini process, but if you stay determined and focused, you will work through those feelings and dramatic times to reach a peaceful and stable future. Basing your practice on what you need to achieve from it is like having a map or compass that guides you through the process. Solidifying your goal at the beginning will help you create an internal timetable and make clear measurements for progress. Draw up a timetable for daily meditation time, start a journal of your progress, and visualize yourself where you want to be.

When your kundalini awakens, it will be like you've thrown a switch and have instant clarity about the world. You'll better understand the world and everyone and what they mean to you. You'll know yourself better and be more in touch with your natural energies and abilities.

Kundalini gives you a whole new perspective on life and can lead you to an unexpected or wondrous place. It's like looking at the world in multiple dimensions when everything in your life up to now has been in two dimensions. You'll have no doubt what to do or say because you'll know what to do and be guided by your inner voice. With that voice you trust, you'll gain the confidence to make choices that will lead you to where you want to go.

How to Use your Powers

An adage goes, "with great power comes great responsibility." However, with your newfound powers comes the ability to act on them. You will have become a living representation of all energy in your universe, and you'll act as an amplifier of the collective energy of humanity. Some yogis believe the ability to choose, influence others, and affect outcomes can be channeled into positive acts or turned negatively toward others. To harness your power for good, you need to know how to harness the power of your mind, body, and spirit.

The best way to harness your newfound powers is to use them for good. Instead of using your energy for negative thoughts or actions, use it to heal yourself and others. That positive energy will radiate out of you and help heal others. You'll need to recharge your energy daily when moving through the healing process after kundalini awakening. You can take time for meditation or go to yoga, but make sure you have time for introspection and self-analysis. You can write one of these times into your timetable and ask a trusted friend or counsel to help you through the process.

As you work your way through the healing and awakening process, you'll notice that there will be more synchronicities around you. These will occur at the most unexpected and opportune moments. You may even notice new sounds, like voices or musical tones, you may not hear every day.

You may see or experience new smells that don't appear every day. These occurrences will be similar to what a clairvoyant experience. This vision or hearing can happen at will and can happen consciously or subconsciously. Those who believe in the prophetic powers of visions may find these to be incredibly useful in interpreting the future.

What Negative Effects Can Kundalini Awakening Bring?

During your kundalini awakening, you may experience time as slower or slower, and you may react slower to the world around you. There is a possibility you can become stressed or confused if you try to rush the process. This can also lead to depression. Any other aspects of your life may also change, physical and emotional, so you should have patience and resilience as you learn to shift and grow through the process. If you find the awakening process overwhelming or feel out of control, seek the help of a professional who can help see you through the experience.

Helping Someone Experiencing Kundalini Awakening

You can do several things to help someone experiencing kundalini awakening, though you should wait until they are self-actualized before offering assistance. During this time, the kundalini process should remain secret. You can suggest joining them on long walks, meditating together, and going to the summit together if your relationship allows it.

Another way you can help is to agree with them that what is happening is real and not fear it. This is fundamental to overcoming kundalini awakening fears. Do not water down myths as Kundalini becomes more widely known. Remember, scientific discoveries are not based on myth or fact; myths are based more on personal history and experiences than real evidence.

Kundalini awakening is not a mystical experience but a spiritual one that comes to you through your connection to your personal energy. As you become more aware of yourself, you'll become more in tune with your spirituality.

Establishing Daily Routines for your Kundalini Health

If you're skeptical about kundalini awakening, try meditating on kundalini awakening to see if you get any guidance. Connecting yourself, your guides, and your Kundalini can help you awaken your hidden power sources.

As your daily routine becomes more complex and oriented toward health, you begin meditating and practicing yoga, change your diet to be healthier or for higher vibration, and make other changes in your life. Over time, you'll see more epiphanies and clarity about your path. With time, you'll develop wisdom about what to read and what to believe. You should not research stories of kundalini awakening but look for stories of people who have awakened under the scientific method and done the research behind what they teach.

The more you meditate and know yourself as a high-frequency source of spirituality and energy, the more you can open up to the idea of kundalini awakening. I encourage you to spend time researching it for yourself instead of accepting it just because it is new to you.

Kundalini awakening can aid in healing injuries, improve mental health and emotional stability, boost the immune system, and improve respiratory and other functions essential to your health. It should not conflict with your other spiritual exploration methods. It can exist in the absence of faith and can be combined with various other spiritual expressions.

You should not try to force your Kundalini to do anything. Begin by meditating daily, incorporating yoga and exercise whenever possible, and then gradually incorporate other strategies as you see fit. You will know when you feel that the Kundalini is awakening within you; when it does, you will be able to recognize it.

You may want to be more patient with your coworkers or take a mental health day when your kundalini is awakening. Check to see if anything has changed after you grounded yourself in your goals and truth.

If you have a family and are concerned that your kundalini awakening will interfere with family time, schedule your meditations for times when you can be alone and communicate about what you're experiencing. Remember to be patient with yourself rather than applying force to your awakening.

Kundalini awakening will give you some surprising revelations about the nature of your existence and show you that your life matters. Just as the universe knows you and wants you to awaken, you know yourself and feel pulled toward more spirituality. Many ancient texts have referred to Kundalini as a universal consciousness; you should meditate on the ancients' words to learn what it is and why some believe practices such as yoga can change your consciousness.

Using Kundalini Journeys to Flourish

The metaphor of the spiritual path as a journey can serve as inspiration for life. We are often told stories of epic journeys. As you gain knowledge about kundalini awakening, you may find similar adventures in your spiritual journey toward self-actualization. Your spiritual map will include goals, realizations, and epiphanies that will bring you to an understanding of your destiny.

Your kundalini awakening will also offer an opportunity for you to travel and expand your own consciousness. Traveling will not only expand your knowledge base but will also expand your DNA, allowing your body to interact with different types of energies. This can allow you to begin to master other types of reality that have been much too difficult for you to interact with. As you can open up to energies, become one with the universe, and travel to other planes of existence, you can reflect on these travels in your memoir.

Keep a journal of your awakening experiences and maybe even your meditative journeys, and interpret the contents through documents people host online. As you look back on these experiences, you can consider just how they changed you as a person. Take notes of epiphanies, insights, and realizations so that you have something to reference later.

Consider your actions and use the past outcome as a motivating teacher moving forward if you had an awakening start and stop in the past. Discuss with your friends, family, or mentors how your actions affected the outcome and what you learned from the experience.

As you travel and explore your spiritual consciousness, you can combine your experience with spiritual thought to determine what you have learned. Those who blog about their spiritual awakenings often describe similar stages and revelations that others can reference in their spiritual awakenings.

As long as you don't overdo it, exercise can help with kundalini awakening. Physical activity assists the body in processing trauma scars. It can also assist you in achieving recharged energy levels and help your body experience higher vibrations. As you spend more time in the present moment, exercise can cause you to become grounded and present.

Overcoming Fear with Higher Spiritual Knowledge and Adventures

As you travel on the spiritual path, you may wonder if everything you've learned is learned or just a figment of your imagination. Part of your spiritual awakening will be learning the difference between fantasy and reality; doing so will allow you to focus on what you want to achieve rather than what you fear.

Awakening is never complete, but the individual will act and be kinder to everyone, more open to friendliness, and more interested in higher-vibration conversation and food as a result of the process. Your spiritual journey is not measured strictly by the number of epiphanies you have during meditation; rather, those epiphanies will become more subtle over time. As you spend more time on the spiritual path, you gain knowledge that allows you to focus your spiritual energy on the things you want to achieve.

As you travel toward spiritual enlightenment, you should resolve to be gentle with yourself and others. As you become more knowledgeable and interested in spirituality and kundalini awakening, you will slowly understand the difference between reality and fantasy. This will help you overcome your fears and see how your spiritual practices can change your attitude. With time, you can move past fear to understand and accept your path.

Yes, you will develop special abilities, but awakening is a lifelong quest to connect with divinity. If all you do is meditate all day, you will never experience the true benefits of your spiritual awakening. Instead, you will fall back to sleep or fall into self-neglect as you focus on nothing but reaching through the spiritual world.

Develop your "spiritual muscles" by engaging in various spiritual practices such as meditation, yoga, travel, exercise, or connecting with nature. Each time you achieve a realization or epiphanies, honor yourself with praise and surprise yourself as you consciously consider where the realization came from. Your brain processes information 40 billion times faster as you meditate; you learn about 1,000 thoughts daily, but you gain insight from only 40 of those thoughts. Your mind is allowed to wander as you meditate; instead of forcing yourself to focus on the spiritual aspects of your thoughts, simply observe your mind and allow your epiphanies to come to you on their own. When you see where the thought came from, you'll better understand yourself and gain a greater chance for understanding and acceptance.

Meditation helps your mind and body prepare for deeper meditation. Do Kundalini meditations whenever you feel ready. Other useful mediations include visualizing the chakras and opening each one up to its masters. The other side of the kundalini is also helpful. Jot down any epiphanies or associated information and then meditate again later.

Trusting your Intuition

When your kundalini rises, it's difficult to do something wrong, but you'll know if something is not right for you because your intuition will let you know it does not feel right. Trust your intuition; run in the opposite direction if something does not seem to fit or feels right. If you take the wrong path and your kundalini awakening stops, you can easily resume your journey in the right direction.

As you connect with your higher self, you may merge with your core being. When contemplating this path, consider every unresolved issue; your spiritual walks can be thematic, allowing you to walk through those unresolved issues. As you meditate on these unresolved issues and experience them as your guides, your thought patterns will change; this process will reveal the reality of those issues and show you what you have learned as you passed them by during your spiritual journey.

As you meditate, you can then reflect on your spiritual journey as you see what you are learning and how it applies to your everyday life. This is the biggest benefit of a spiritual journey; you learn about and appreciate the learnings. As you develop spirituality and focus your strength on your spiritual mentalities and connections, you can make a difference in the world; by merging and integrating with the Universe's divinity, you can help others feel your power and theirs as they share your higher truths.

Take things as they come and gradually introduce new techniques. While you may already have the knowledge to travel spiritually, you may find that you need to push forward or engage more in other practices as you move to the next spiritual level. Each level has different expectations and learning techniques. When you extend yourself and your expectations, you become more self-aware and gain more clarity and strength.

Chapter 4: Kundalini Basics

This chapter will explain the benefits of kundalini awakening and how to recognize your own. Kundalini awakening is a natural process by which the body's energy channels, called nadis, are stimulated to "wake up." Kundalini is symbolized as a coiled snake whose tail rests in the root chakra, and its head rests in the crown of the head. When these channels are awakened, kundalini moves upward and achieves full awakening.

The Advantages of Kundalini Awakening

As we go over these ten benefits of kundalini awakening, remember to be grateful for each one and thankful that these changes are now possible for you. You can now realize a new way of life in which your body, mind, and spirit are brought into alignment with the Divine.

1. The primary reason for kundalini awakening is spiritual awakening. As with other forms of spiritual awakening, kundalini awakens your spiritual consciousness and awareness. You are now capable of experiencing such spiritual states of consciousness as having direct experience with the Divine Source, seeing auras, receiving information and guidance from angels and ascended masters, experiencing heightened intuition, spiritual healing, spiritual creativity and inspiration, and higher states of consciousness and personal growth.
2. When kundalini becomes active, consciousness expands. This expansion of consciousness eventually produces a

kundalini experience in which consciousness is experienced as consciousness without a body. This is referred to as the "kingdom of heaven," a state of consciousness in which all limitations are experienced as non-existence.

3. Kundalini awakening brings spiritual clarity. Spiritual clarity allows you to be more clairaudient, clairvoyant, clairsentient, and claircognizant. In addition, you receive information intuitively and directly, and you can sense the spiritual nature of people and places. In addition, you can now connect with cosmic intelligence and cosmic and angelic beings. These abilities greatly enhance your spiritual and psychic abilities.

4. As kundalini awakens, you experience heightened intuition and find yourself making much more intuitive decisions. Kundalini awakens intuition by grounding intuition into your body. When intuition is grounded in your body, it becomes far more useful and has obvious practical significance.

5. Intuition is extraordinarily useful during kundalini awakening because it allows you to sense Divine guidance more accurately. During kundalini awakening, intuition is one of the most reliable ways of sensing Divine guidance. Divine guidance is typically expressed as feelings and emotions accessible through intuition. With heightened intuition, you are able to experience the presence, guidance, and love of your Divine Source.

6. Kundalini awakening can help protect you from possession by negativities, causing you to have out-of-body experiences while sleeping. When you experience kundalini during your sleep, you experience out-of-body experiences. These out-of-body experiences result from being ejected from the lower astral planes by the kundalini energy. If you experience kundalini awakening

as you sleep, you typically awaken in a completely different area of your home than you normally sleep.

7. As your kundalini begins to move within, your mind will become clearer and more enriched, and your IQ may even rise. With this expansion of mind comes an expansion of compassion and loving-kindness. You will be better able to understand others' perspectives, live from the heart, and make more positive life choices.

8. Many people seek kundalini awakening for personal health reasons. When Kundalini energy is awakened and balanced, the body's energy systems function at an optimal level. As a result, you can counter many physical ailments, such as chronic fatigue, high blood pressure, menstrual cramps, sexual problems, arthritis, etc. Your immune system also becomes more balanced when these energy channels are awakened. As kundalini awakens, the body becomes healthier and more resistant to disease.

9. Kundalini awakening creates psychic abilities like clairaudience, clairvoyance, clairsentience, claircognizance, telepathy, precognition, and healing psychically, which is impossible in "normal" people. These abilities allow people to function more effectively in society and better integrate their spiritual life with their day-to-day experiences.

10. Many seek kundalini awakening for kundalini yoga, a progressive spiritual discipline that speeds up a person's spiritual growth. In particular, kundalini yoga promotes charka balancing, which occurs when the inner and outer chakras are brought into balance.

11. Kundalini awakening increases one's sense of peace, bliss, tranquillity, and faith in the universe. This peace can be felt even when not in nature or meditating.

12. You will also notice patterns and synchronicities and how they can relate to living out your purpose and soul

mission in this lifetime. You will also see the underlying metaphysical principles that govern the Universe and how they affect your life.

13. Kundalini awakening can help you feel younger, stronger, and more attractive and prevent or reverse degenerative brain disorders. Call it divine intervention or simply luck, but a higher state of health often accompanies kundalini awakening.

14. When kundalini is awakened, a person becomes more social and less shy. As a result, many people actively seek out friends and family. The social transformation can be dramatic as you find ways to embrace the changes in your life and start to enjoy being with people again.

15. Even if you start as an atheist, you may find yourself questioning your beliefs as you experience the incredible spiritual experiences that kundalini awakening can provide. The very act of questioning your beliefs can help bring you closer to the truth.

16. Kundalini awakening can result in more intense orgasms and the ability to control and focus this energy, which can result in tantric sex. Living in harmony with the Divine often means a more or less spiritual or intuitive lifestyle. You experience living more consciously and intuitively. As a result, you can use more of your mind and less of your body to live your daily life.

17. As you awaken to spiritual connections and understand your purpose on Earth, you become more inspired to lead a holistic life and design a spiritual practice.

18. As kundalini awakening progresses, you become more magnetically and psychically attractive. The high magnetism and psychic attractiveness lead to improved relationships.

19. As your spiritual awareness and understanding develop, you become more compassionate and loving with others. You experience the soul connection with all beings,

which is universal love. As a result, once negative emotions or attachments that no longer serve you are released, you feel much lighter.

20. This high vibrational energy associated with kundalini is experienced as warmth or heat through your body. This energy often feels very intense near the genitals and hands. Many people experience the "pins and needles" sensation in their extremities as the kundalini opens vortexes of energy along these pathways.

21. One of the 12 universal laws that define the nature of our physical reality is the law of attraction. Kundalini awakening enhances one's ability to attract what they require. As a result, you find that your life changes for the better as you attract more positive people and situations into your life.

22. Kundalini awakening can enhance your meditation and consciousness skills. You can meditate for as long as you wish when Kundalini energy is awakened, the chakras spin, and the energy channels are awakened and balanced.

23. Kundalini awakening can dramatically enhance a woman's ability to conceive and carry a child to term. This partly results from a blend of spirituality with conventional medical care and partly from the power of the sacral chakra. Various medical doctors are currently using kundalini energy to help women conceive and carry a healthy baby to full term.

24. Even people who don't believe in reincarnation often experience life after death.

Many people suffering from chronic illnesses like cancer, life-threatening illnesses, auto-immune disorders, and others will find relief during their kundalini awakening process. Kundalini awakening facilitates healing on the human soul level, where the element of belief is healed and accepted. Kundalini awakening enhances the cleansing process of the body's energy field as well as the physical body. The increased activity of your pineal gland allows more light energy to enter your bloodstream, thus resulting in better sleep and more energy.

There are many myths about kundalini awakening, but it can be a beneficial experience for many people. Before moving forward unknowingly, it's a good idea to figure out what's true and what's not. Kundalini awakening is both safe and beneficial. People crying or having muscle spasms may appear strange, but the energy released is healthy, natural, and enlightening.

Your relationships with these people should not suffer due to your awakening. Instead, your patience and understanding of them should grow, which will benefit your relationship.

Kundalini awakening should always include both physical and spiritual elements, movement and breath, yoga and meditation, and so on so that the mind, body, and soul can all be awakened at the same time. Awakening is simple; persistence, commitment, determination, and focus are all it takes. If you're having trouble, consider your wounds, traumas, and scars, and consider seeing a therapist.

While Reiki and Kundalini awakening may be inextricably linked, they are not. You can practice Reiki for years without ever experiencing kundalini awakening. This process will not transform you into a superhero or make you superhuman. It will, however, unlock your psychic abilities, which aren't as unusual for humans as we might think.

Kundalini Awakening Signs

Many strange symptoms will likely occur as you begin the process of Kundalini awakening, but this is normal. While severe

Kundalini symptoms are rare, they can occur. Some of the most common symptoms are:

- Episodes of shaking, trembling, or spasms. Awakening usually involves some degree of shaking and trembling, accompanied by shakiness in the hands or hands grasping for balance. These symptoms may be very mild or quite severe.
- Often, as awakened Kundalini rises from the root chakra to the heart chakra, you may experience many of the emotions associated with the root chakra. They may be experienced as anger, fear, grief, sadness, or as you should with Kundalini experience grief or sadness, you may experience difficult feelings of frustration toward a person or emotional upset related to the loss of a relationship or job or similar. These feelings are a normal part of the process of awakening.
- Feelings of bliss, deep gratitude or profound happiness and calm are common Kundalini experiences. You may feel completely weightless and experience intense pleasure. Perhaps even more commonly, you may simply feel completely relaxed. While this energy is not often experienced as sexual energy, some people may experience this type of energy during Kundalini awakening. You may experience more sensual and sexual feelings during these periods.
- As your Kundalini awakens, you may experience extreme hot and cold flashes. You may feel faint and dizzy. You may overheat or shiver. You may feel cold, and your skin suddenly turns red as overheating. As this happens around your body, you may feel dizzy, faint, and confused. You may feel confused, off balance, or like you will not be able to move.
- Some people experience severe anger and irritability as Kundalini flows up the spine. You may feel angry at the

unfairness of life. These expressions are part of the healing process and require you to move through these feelings.

- You will have extremely creative periods when you work through sacral chakra blockages. These are evidence of awakening. However, the blocks may return, especially if you neglect your psychological health during these times.
- You may feel deeply spiritual and connected to all things. Others may not recognize or understand these feelings. You may feel that nobody understands your experience. Cleansing and detoxing of energy are also common during the awakening process. You may experience painful detoxing experiences as old energy leaves the body.
- You may feel intensely aware of what's happening around and in your body. You may feel as if your entire body is vibrating and pulsating with energy, and as a result, you may tend to touch objects around you more and move slowly and carefully in the world, especially while entering a new
- You will feel more "pure" and connected to all aspects of divinity as you cleanse your chakras of toxicity and dirt. You may feel like all is pure light in your heart and soul and less dense energy with the understanding that it is a blush of divinity that can get lost in the process of living. Many people feel that the world gets smaller when chakras are awakened, as you may feel that you are part of the universe or that all is alive and connected through your embodied experience with the world. This can take some people by surprise, especially if they have been raised to believe the opposite.
- Because blockages manifest as problematic or negative personality traits, many people work out personality kinks when their kundalinis are awakened. Kundalini energy flows through the nervous system, and your

nervous system activates when you feel threatened. This is why people sometimes undergo a personality shift during spiritual awakening.

- Perhaps you feel a little off or notice your energy feels a little off. Maybe you feel less motivated or focused than usual. Perhaps you're experiencing physical issues, like headaches or body pain, that you never expected. If you've been experiencing a slump in your creative motivation, it's a sign that you're on the verge of awakening.

Chapter 5: How to Awaken Your Kundalini

This chapter contains techniques for experiencing kundalini awakening and 6 additional methods to enhance your experience. Kundalini Awakening is a distinctly positive human experience. It is much like an epiphany where an individual suddenly understands something on a deeply symbolic level that one had not understood previously. This understanding can range from cellular understandings, such as how our body regulates its temperature and immune system, to spiritual truths about the intrinsic unity of all life and the Source from which it all arises.

1. Kundalini Awakening is the experience of the life force or prana awakening the serpent at the bottom of the spine and opening the third eye. This is much more profound than waking us from a normal dream state into a deep sleep because kundalini awakening permanently changes our consciousness and awareness. Kundalini Awakening occurs spontaneously in moments of great emotion or intense meditation and is usually accompanied by intense sensations from the base of the spine up to the head.

2. Kundalini yoga is the best place to start if you want to work on kundalini awakening because it helps you work through chakra blockages and activates the kundalini. While you can use yoga to explore the spiritual experiences of kundalini awakening, you can experience kundalini awakening without distinguishing whether you are in yoga postures in your sleep or while meditating. Many people require assistance in detaching from the distractions of the mind and the world to focus

sufficiently to visualize the intricate inner movements of the Kundalini. Meditation with a guide can help with this. This kundalini awakening technique involves shifting your focus from the root to the crown chakra and back again, then allowing the kundalini to fall down with the magnet replaced.

3. There are a few unintentional roadblocks that many kundalini practitioners face. You'll want to reject as many negative influences in your life as possible and work to transform your personality traits into their opposite extreme of expression.

4. If you are frequently the center of attention, try to be more subtle in public. Instead of focusing on your own needs and desires, observe who rises and listens to what they have to say. Traditional kundalini awakening elements include combining mind and body through chanting and singing. This mind-body alignment is very beneficial for the flow of shakti energy through your system, and it will also help practitioners experiencing throat chakra blockages.

5. Consider what you liked to do for fun when you were a kid. Consider what makes you happy and whether you are still striving to achieve those goals or have given up on them for various reasons. If you have difficulty going with the flow, it is possible that your solar plexus chakra is blocked, imbalanced, or spinning in the wrong direction. If you say "yes" more frequently, your kundalini will know what to do.

6. Some people are too easygoing and can't help but get caught up in the flow, making it difficult for them to say "no" when it counts. To regain strength and boost your soul, practice saying "no" whenever you'd normally be "pushed over." By cultivating your willpower, you will make it easier to say no to anything that detracts from your soul's growth.

7. Kundalini awakening primarily involves forgetting concepts, ideas, and beliefs that separate the practitioner from the soul. It is important to practice daily meditation on these deeper levels of experience so that they become part of your consciousness so that you don't think about them or even notice them. Relax and focus on the kundalini energy as it flows in all your chakras and back again.

8. Music therapy is a doctor-approved technique for any type of psychological or spiritual awakening. You can use music to process anything, and if you experience any spontaneous hot or cold flashes, emotional outbursts, or laughing bursts, you're on the right track.

9. Instead of music or sound, you could use art to awaken your Kundalini. You could also start making your own art again, no matter how deeply you've buried it. The intuitive part of you awake during kundalini awakening can sketch on canvas or a mug of coffee, sand, or fabric.

10. Nature reminds us of our true nature with its beauty, symmetry, and oneness. Because many people have gotten out of touch with nature, it is easy to feel separated from it. But kundalini awakening allows us to see nature's beauty, symmetry, and oneness in ourselves.

11. Colors have wavelengths and vibrations that heal us, sometimes without our knowledge. Colors can help cleanse or open chakras, but they can also help us heal in ways we are unaware of. Like how chakras have corresponding colors, our aura becomes brighter as your Kundalini approaches awakening. Stimulating the prana or life force in the body through mantras, breath, music, and movement can help open the chakras and awaken the Kundalini when practiced chronically. Musical waves that resonate with the energy centers can help activate Kundalini, Shakti, and chakras. Because kundalini awakening is not just about focusing on chakras, it is

important to consider music, sound, vibrations, and mantras from all perspectives.

12. Less time spent on technology is preferable. You will become more sensitive as you open up and experience kundalini awakening, and this sensitivity can have disastrous consequences for your awakening goals. You can use one type of social media to get a little bit of everything you might need and then drastically reduce your weekly posts. Then, refresh your social media feed by purging your friend list, hashtags you follow, and pages you like.

13. You must begin to look for synchronicities in your life and trust the world around you for your healing and growth. This will assist you in quickly relearning how to trust and make substantial life changes.

14. When you start meditating, you'll notice your breathing more than ever, and your kundalini will respond to this increased awareness. Breathe deeply into your stomach and imagine a small serpent sleeping in the pit of your stomach.

15. The kundalini serpent ascends from the root chakra to the sacral, solar plexus, heart, throat, third eye, and crown chakras before descending and repeating its journey. Consider which chakras are blocked if you have difficulty maintaining proper posture.

16. Focus your energy on the root chakra during your daily meditation, breathe into your belly, and feel the vibration there. Then, chant your mantra or simply "ohm" several times to open the entire chakra channel within you.

17. Instead of shutting yourself down, becoming angry at everything, or shutting down when you are upset, try to reshape your perspective on the world and see the evidence of divinity in every experience, challenge, advantage, situation, and exchange.

18. If you don't know who your spirit guides are yet, do some spiritual research and see if your guides will appear. You can then approach them for assistance with your Kundalini awakening.

19. Holding healing crystals around you can increase your capacity for patience, love, devotion, trust, and so on. These earth minerals have a vibration and a life essence, and they can align and cleanse all seven chakras at the same time.

20. You can activate Kundalini by paying it forward, performing random acts of kindness, and watching what comes back to you. These practices may eventually become second nature to you, or they may even bring you material benefits.

21. If you're a regular meditator, try beginning your day with a chakra cleanse. Imagine your inner peace and wholeness after this cleansing is complete, and imagine your chakras becoming more aligned with each shower.

22. Grudges are spiritually toxic, but they can be healed by active and radical expressions of love, patience, and forgiveness. When you are butting up against your grudges, try to be the better person and reject the grudge.

23. Kundalini awakening is not about sex; some sexual practices can help your kundalini rise and increase your shakti. Tantric sex is one of the most beneficial and productive sexual practices associated with Kundalini awakening. If you have frequent orgasms but don't yet understand tantric sex, you can try focusing your orgasmic energy upwards through your chakras to your crown to initiate awakening.

More Ways to Awaken

In addition to these Kundalini boosters, you can add more intensive practices to your daily routine to strengthen and intensify the experience. Here are a few more steps that you can use to awaken your Kundalini energy:

- If you are physically capable of doing so, you should begin running to improve your strength, endurance, and alignment. If you find that running causes you undue stress, you should cut it out of your routine. Instead, switch to walking or swimming.
- Eat vibrationally powerful food if you want to awaken the source of subtle yet universal energy within you. Replace processed foods with whole foods; your cells will replenish themselves with the nutrients in these healthier foods.
- Don't forget to get outside as you begin this life-changing practice! Nature is a never-ending source of subtle physical healing energies as well as a plethora of signs that can assist you in communicating with your guides, higher self, and intuition.
- As your chakras open up and you experience Kundalini awakening, you will be forced to confront your shortcomings, including your inability to love purely and selflessly. Putting yourself in a service-oriented job will strengthen your ability to love others.
- Working with subtle energy-healing modalities will teach you that your intuition is more powerful and useful than anything else. These techniques can also help you open chakras more quickly by projecting light energy through them.
- When you begin focusing your Kundalini awakening practices consciously and deliberately, your body and mind will become more in tune with your spirit. You will start to experience spiritual visions and hear the voices

of your guides and angels more frequently. You may start to see auras when you meditate or look deeply into another person's eyes.

- As you dedicate time to improving your spiritual self, people around you will notice the changes and sometimes even misinterpret them. Avoid arguing with people over these spiritual changes to help foster and maintain your positivity and energy.

- Flower essences can help with Kundalini awakening by placing a few buds of a specific flower in a clear bowl of water and leaving it in the sun for 12 hours. You can then take the essence orally to treat various ailments.

- Reiki healing is a Japanese energy work technique that uses the practitioner's insight and potential power to remove obstructions and blockages within the individual. It can be done from a distance and does not have to be accompanied by a massage.

- Massages can aid in blockage release with or without adding Reiki. Massages feel good on your skin and muscles and can help you become more aware of any blockages you may have.

- If you're comfortable doing so, you can still seek art therapy. Art and music therapy are great places to start; if you can't afford a personal doctor, you can develop your own therapies. This may seem like a lot to learn and practice, but Kundalini awakening can improve your life in every way just by being more conscious. The more awake you are, the less you will fear and enjoy the present moment.

- You can stimulate Kundalini with essential oils or herbal healing, and you can also forage for plants with a guidebook if you prefer a more hands-on, low-tech approach. Your meditation space should inspire, restore your energy, and stimulate your chakras. Find a space that inspires you and makes you feel relaxed; a clean, dark room works well. If you meditate outside, look for places with low lighting and no disturbing noises.

- Try sun gazing to decalcify your pineal gland and reprogram your energy using the sun's energy. Sun exposure has anti-aging, anti-hunger, and anti-illness properties. It is also great for overall mental clarity and well-being.
- You could try homeopathic remedies to get to the bottom of what's causing those chakra blockages in the first place. Homeopathic remedies are made from the vibrational essences of plants, minerals, and animals to alleviate debilitating conditions or illnesses.
- Instead of running if you're having trouble with your lower chakra regions, try taking a dance class. The Kundalini will be inspired by movement, and every rhythmically planned step you take will only serve to align your life more.

Kundalini awakening is subtle, powerful, and life-changing. When you begin practicing these Kundalini boosters regularly, you will be amazed at the results you can achieve within a few months. If you are experiencing difficulty sleeping, anxiety, depression, or disease, you may wake up feeling happier and more energetic than you ever have in your life.

Chapter 6: Fixing your Awakened State

This chapter will assist you if your Kundalini awakening is not progressing as expected. We will investigate three different themes that could affect your process and potential dangers and risks that could interfere.

As one ascends through the chakras, various types and intensities of energies are released and facilitated. These are normally experienced as blissful experiences or states of consciousness which energize our physical body and being. However, as you pass through a particular chakra, it may activate new dimensions or ranges of consciousness within yourself that produce new states of experience. These new states of subconsciousness exist within and are independent of the chakra energy they are created in. Therefore, a chakra may be activated at a very high level during Kundalini awakening yet produce much lower states of consciousness depending on how high or low an individual's consciousness is.

Many things could be holding you back on your journey, but this section will help you realize what can help. A lack of proper grounding could be a major factor holding you back and obstructing your Kundalini awakening process. As explained earlier, this process requires intense energetic activation and circulation throughout the body. Therefore, going outside and connecting to some physical foundation is necessary before attempting to ascend your Kundalini energy. This is why meditation is so important. However, many were not grounded when they began their Kundalini awakening process.

Consciousness must be present to have a conscious experience of anything. Many people have no conscious awareness of their Kundalini moving through them, yet they are nevertheless experiencing some type of energy movement. Unfortunately, many of our emotions and mental energies can interfere with the processes of the Kundalini. Emotions such as anger or fear can interfere with your emotional energy field and negatively affect it. On the other hand, the higher emotional energy centers, like the heart and the throat, can be positively affected by love or wisdom energies and positively reflect these energies back onto receptive ones.

Many people can't handle such intense energies being activated within them or their energy field. Consider that a normal fire can generate intense heat; the same can be said for light or electricity. People are usually aware of the heat fires generate, but if they look closely, they can detect the "live" current of electricity flowing within. The flow of electricity is stronger and much more intense than the heat generated.

Sometimes our bodies aren't quite ready for Kundalini awakening, and that's fine. You will reach a point in your healing where you can handle Kundalini awakening on top of everything else, which is fine. Energies that resonate within and stimulate our chakras to affect our physical bodies, even when we're unaware they're doing so! For example, if you listen to certain music, you may notice your body responding in ways you did not expect. If you feel angry while listening to one style, you may feel the need to destroy something or harm your body in some way; whereas if you listen to another style, you may feel more calm, relaxed, peaceful, or uplifted.

The Kundalini awakening process may be much faster and even too intense for people who have unblocked chakras. To slow things down, try to meditate every other day. If that doesn't help, try meditating only once or every other week. Try to complement your meditation with a few prayer sessions per week. If possible, give yourself a rest period at the end of each chakra sequence, then begin the next sequence three to six months later. As you progress through the chakras, you experience various states of mind.

Some may find it difficult to believe, but your diet may impede your awakening. Begin by eating fewer processed foods and more fruits and vegetables. Eat smaller meals throughout the day and avoid eating within two to three hours of sleep. Eat plenty of almonds, walnuts, sunflower seeds, pumpkin seeds, and pistachios. Drink plenty of water daily and avoid drinking sodas or juices with added sugars. These simple suggestions should help you get on your way to feeling healthier.

Some issues with Kundalini awakening are rooted in the individual's ability to focus. You can easily correct these issues by focusing your energy when you meditate on your heart, belly, and gut. Performing this meditation for several minutes daily can help with a lack of focus and balance, strengthen the inner body chakras, and allow the Kundalini awakening to progress.

In terms of spiritual development, some individuals can see auras and people's spiritual bodies due to their Kundalini energy. There is no scientific evidence that suggests that people in higher states of spiritual development, including being awakened, can see auras more easily and with more precision than

Awakening can be difficult because you will be forced to confront and change your flaws. These self-based reality checks cause some people to stumble in their awakening process. Remember: You are always being guided and directed on your life path. If you stumble or fall, get up and try again. Do not give up. Remember you are healing your soul's wounds and your physical body.

Physical discomforts and emotional issues can cause you to stumble in your Kundalini awakening process. Every action reacts, and you are also healing many physical, mental, and emotional wounds by going through this healing. Healing from these wounds is necessary for your Kundalini awakening to proceed. Without healing, your Kundalini.

If your friends and family dismiss your Kundalini awakening efforts, don't get too down on yourself just yet. You can always try again with different tactics the next time, or you can use the information to create your own supportive community. Some environments are incompatible with one's quest for enlightenment. If it feels unsafe to meditate or practice yoga in a particular location, find another until you're strong enough to combat that vibe.

Awakening Possibilities and Risks

Some risks are associated with Kundalini awakening, especially going for more than you can handle. The main reason people experience problems is that the Kundalini energy is awakened too quickly, and the person is not prepared to handle the energy.

It's not unusual for Kundalini energy to be awakened with the force of a tidal wave. Some people may experience severe physical reactions, even to the point of hospitalization, due to pain, vomiting, etc. This is why it is important not to awaken your Kundalini energy too quickly or without first being grounded and properly preparing yourself energetically.

Some also have vivid dreams at night, visions during the day, and experience strong sexual feelings during the awakening process. Others see colors around themselves, experience sudden changes in emotions or sensations, or feel their bodies quivering with a sense of life that is new to them. All these symptoms are common and are not life-threatening or damaging in and of themselves.

A great deal of spiritual practice is needed to safely and properly awaken the Kundalini energy. By keeping yourself grounded and balanced, your Kundalini energy will flow smoothly and safely for you. Kundalini awakening enhances your spiritual development because it causes you to expand your consciousness to an increasingly higher and more subtle state of existence.

The danger of spiritual overexertion is very real. After weeks and months of focusing too much energy on one chakra, you may burn out and feel like you should take a break. Rather than ignoring the need for rest, it is more important to try to rest and relax for a few days so that you don't damage your psyche or even harm your body. The best strategy is to take things as they come rather than attempting to do too much at once.

Many people feel anger and resentment when they go through spiritual awakenings. This anger is usually directed at them for doubting their abilities or for not being able to let go of old habits or thought patterns. Shadow work focuses on releasing this anger and helping you see your truth in healthier ways so that you can work with it instead of against it.

It is common to experience certain physical changes during Kundalini awakening. For example, you may find your thyroid functioning differently or begin to experience bouts of anxiety, energy surges, and unexpected headaches. All these things can occur if you work too hard or push yourself too hard through the awakening process. You must perform Kundalini meditations for about 20-30 minutes a day rather than trying to meditate for longer periods.

There is an equal risk for those who attempt to do too much and too quickly, as forced and accelerated Kundalini damages the system and creates additional states of disease in the chakras. Therefore, do not try to force the process. Taking it easy and working with the natural energy flow is better. If you're doing too much and too quickly, your body will most likely be unable to keep up with the speed that your mind can handle. Yoga and other body-based practices can help you balance your practice.

You may feel spiritually "high" and less grounded in your earthen body as your Kundalini awakens. Many people feel disconnected from their bodies and find it easy to become obsessed or attached to their spiritual growth. It's important not to lose touch with your physical body as you grow spiritually and to experience the joy and lightness you feel in your soul. When this happens, take a deep breath, imagine a cord falling from your navel to the earth, and ground yourself.

Part of being in a state of heightened consciousness is waking up at odd hours or losing sleep due to insomnia. If you have a passion for spirituality, you are already very sensitive and have probably experienced a pattern of getting little sleep and little rest. This lifestyle can be difficult to change if you identify strongly with your passions. Take time daily to meditate and do yoga to help your body rest and release stress, anxiety, and toxins.

Many people will experience jerkiness and muscle spasms during the Kundalini awakening process. The muscles around your spine, neck, arms, and legs may twitch when you first experience higher vibrations. This is a natural part of being awakened. As your body adjusts to the energy flow, these spasms will cause less discomfort and irritation. Take deep breaths and try to relax; these are natural "growing pains" associated with awakening.

When you confront your flaws and realize you can only go up, you may feel lost and question everything you thought was true, real, and good. Keep an eye on anyone you know attempting to awaken their Kundalini.

When you awaken, you may not realize everything that needs to change. People may struggle to adjust to the new worldview. People who hold traditional religious views may also struggle to come to terms with Kundalini awakening because this forces them to abandon their old beliefs for something new.

Not everyone is receptive to spiritual awakening; some may fear or reject it. They will either attempt to keep you from exploring spiritually or risk making you uncomfortable by trying to control the spiritual growth process. Although it may be difficult to hear negative comments and come from a place of love and compassion, you must practice tolerance and respect through all the ups and downs of your spiritual journey.

When your Kundalini awakens, anyone who has experienced trauma will be guided to work through those wounds and scars, which can mean a lot of intimidating work. However, if you can deal with the pain and work with your wounded self rather than around it, and if you believe in your ability to heal, the pain eventually dissipates.

You may feel alone and isolated during the spiritual awakening process because you don't identify with your physical reality, and you may feel alienated from others who may see you as different or inferior to them. You may experience spiritual and physical attacks from people afraid of the changes you see in yourself. They may lash out at you or even pressure you to return to your old behaviors or beliefs.

If your Kundalini rises, you may be drawn to ayahuasca ceremonies or excessive marijuana use. Be aware that these sessions are not without repercussions. Ayahuasca ceremonies can lead you to disconnect from reality. Marijuana alters your mental state and your ability to concentrate or see things. It can also affect your decision-making ability because marijuana harms your brain's frontal lobe. Being highly charged and having extremely heightened energy stimulates the mind, emotions, and physical body. When you meditate and center yourself, you are using your energy effectively rather than wasting it. However, keep things in check on the inside by using drugs as little or none as possible during your awakening.

Chapter 7: Kundalini Disorders

Kundalini syndrome is an unpleasant syndrome that can occur in some awakening practitioners. Therefore, what happens is that the Kundalini energy rises, but the energy gets stuck somewhere in the energy system. This would cause blockages in the energy system, preventing the energy from flowing freely in the practitioner's area. It can appear as constant jitters and anxiety accompanied by so-called "delusions of grandeur."

Many people have gone through the Kundalini awakening process, and some have failed. Failure is mainly due to the inability to handle the super-conscious and unconscious mind that goes hand in hand with the Kundalini awakening experience.

The unconscious mind can manifest as anger, anxiety, panic attacks, depression, and more if it remains unconscious and untrained. You must train the conscious mind to deal with the unconscious mind until the energy is no longer stuck. When there is a blockage in the energy system, the blocked energy would be responsible for the manifestation of disorders of the mind and the spirit. It is manifested in the form of delusions and hallucinations, bodily disorders in the form of pain, nausea, or flu-like symptoms, and disorder of the spirit in the form of undue attachment to the awakening experience itself.

Overcoming blockages is what the awakening is about, and this is why the Kundalini energy rises in the first place. To release the blockage, you must train the awareness to not only listen to the mind but also to the intuition or the super-conscious mind.

The super-conscious mind is higher than the conscious mind, which is in charge when the body sleeps.

The super-conscious mind sees beyond the conscious mind. Once this higher awareness is developed, You can overcome the blockages in the system. When this happens, you will awaken more and more Kundalini energy through time until the person is spiritually awakened in full consciousness.

Other reasons can be from using psychedelic drugs during the process, using too much alcohol or drugs, and stressing the physical body. People who take too much LSD or Ayahuasca during the awakening process may have received too much kundalini energy causing them to experience too much activation at once. This abuse can cause a blockage in the system, causing the kundalini energies to stay dormant or stuck for a long time. This block could happen if the person is not trained and adept at handling the mind and emotions.

Similarly, too much alcohol and drugs in the system will cause the glandular system to scramble the hormones in your physical body. When this happens, your physical body won't be able to handle too much glandular stimulation at once, which can cause the awakening process to be difficult. Stressing the physical body also can cause a block in your system and prevent the flow of energy from manifesting healthily.

For people who are living a carnal life, they won't be able to experience the process of the kundalini awakenings fully. This is because the performance of a sensual life requires one to remain conscious and not connected to the superconscious mind. A sexual life is one where the person lives only in the body and mind, not the mind, body, and soul. There is no consciousness to speak of when one is in a sensual life.

Ego vs. Awakening

You have fallen into an ego trap if you differentiate yourself from others. In the process of awakening, competition with others is not a requirement. All forms of comparison will only confuse and decrease the personal power of the awakening process. Your ego will only make the process of awakening more painful and harmful to you. Keep your ego in check and evolve at your own pace, for you are the only one who can decide when to awaken. So do your part and keep the ego in check. Don't be envious of those ahead of you in the process. When you compare yourself to others, you are wasting valuable personal energy that you could use for your very own spiritual growth.

Kundalini awakening is a process that requires ancillary methods to help you succeed during the awakening process. If you rely too much on yoga alone, you might not be able to succeed during the process. Yoga is useful in calming your mind and body so that you will be protected from the unknown torments that the unconscious mind can unleash, but to achieve a full awakening process, you must learn how to fully take care of your mind, body, and soul. These techniques include meditation, qi gong, breathing exercises, dietary changes, etc.

If you seek to gain spiritual knowledge and enlightenment and being spiritually awakened is not enough, then you are not thinking deeply enough about it. Sometimes, people seek spiritual enlightenment for the wrong reasons. Sometimes they want to improve their self-esteem and self-worth. Sometimes they want to achieve fame or gains at the expense of others. Sometimes they want to become famous spiritually, which is a selfish desire. There are many wrong reasons to seek spiritual enlightenment or awakening, and they all stem from the egoistic mind or the selfish mind.

The ego is a selfish mind that feeds the person's self-centered desires. Once one loses control of the egoistic and selfish mind, the person would fall into the wrong reasons to seek enlightenment and not become spiritually awakened. When this occurs, the person would even think and perform actions out of self-interest. The egoistic mind is the most selfish mind that one can possess. Once you awaken from the egoistic mind, the person will see yourself as having nothing to offer others. You would not be ready to learn and evolve spiritually at that point, but only when the spirit of selflessness leaves the mind.

You've fallen into another ego trap if you compare yourself to others based on who is more spiritual than who. Others are more spiritually awakened than you, but it doesn't mean that it shouldn't spiritually awaken you. All types of spiritual awakening are equally important, and it doesn't matter if you are more awakened than someone else if you are both spiritually awakened. A spiritual awakening will give you so much joy in your life that it won't even matter what benefits you can gain from it.

True spirituality seeks to balance the ego and the soul. If you compare yourself to other awakened people based on who has the purest love vibration, let go of your judgment and remember the importance of balance in all things.

Post-awakening Effects

Reconsider the concept of good and bad and stop projecting it onto others. To achieve the awakening of your Kundalini, you can impose different kinds of penances on your body by increasing your discipline. You can walk on coals without flinching, endure hunger, or drink poisonous concoctions without fear. You can do this all unto yourself, and in so doing, you will also achieve enlightenment in a deeper sense.

In the awakening process, you will feel different sensations in your body, and you might think you are not thinking anymore. This is normal and happens to everyone during the awakening process. There are many things that one can do during the awakening process to help calm the mind and allow it to deal with the clearing of the energy.

Spiritual awakening does not only mean that you can manifest supernatural powers or that you live longer. However, these are some benefits that a spiritual awakening can give you. It also means you can become a better person and treat other beings better. The benefits of spiritual awakening will manifest after a spiritual awakening but before the Kundalini is fully activated. This is when the dormant energies of the Kundalini are awakened and freed, which is the time to experience the first mental breakthrough of the Kundalini begin to awaken. Once the Kundalini is fully opened, the person has matured spiritually and can use their inner energy to its fullest extent.

People will look to you for assistance and guidance as you progress toward awakening. Insincere niceness will turn people off until it is transformed into something more productive. Your newfound power can hurt or help people out of difficult situations, and you must learn to control these powers properly. But do not be blinded or fooled by people's selfish motives or agendas.

Any judgmental comparison you make will be proof of a major blunder on your part. As you progress deeper into awakening, begin to notice your thought patterns. What are you thinking? Are you distracting yourself with gossip? Are you stuck in your ego or collecting new material? Do you envy other people's successes? Are you comparing yourself to others who seem more advanced than you? Stop all these thinking patterns immediately, or they will keep you from becoming fully awakened.

Patience is a Must

Many pieces of advice in this chapter warn you not to rush your awakening. Allow patience and proper timing to enter your process, and remember what awakening is all about. Awakening is about love and helping others, not criticizing or comparing yourself to others.

Spiritual awakening and enlightenment are also about being a better person in all your actions and behaviors. Be more alert and aware of your words and actions. Do not let ego or fear dominate you and cloud your judgment; always seek the truth's knowledge. True spirituality is loving thy neighbor as thyself, and it does not imply you should act unlovingly to other people.

Kundalini awakening should not be rushed, and you should do practices regularly. Maintain your focus throughout the process, and schedule your meditation and yoga sessions accordingly. Channel your energy properly, and do not be distracted by your life's duties. Only when your energy is fully unleashed will you be truly awakened.

The Midst and Purpose of Kundalini Awakening

One of the most common kundalini awakening mistakes involves one's mindset and setting, and one should spend time in nature weekly during the awakening process. Natural surroundings play a vital role in the yoga and kundalini awakening process, and spending time here will also cleanse and purify your being. However, many do it for a brief time. Try to meditate in nature as much as possible, especially if you are afraid of being alone. Allow the peacefulness and serenity of nature to help calm your mind. This also helps you focus on something and teaches you how to accomplish what you want in life, which benefits everyone there. Spending time in nature can also escape your busy schedules and make it easier for you to focus better while awake.

Another important tip in yoga and kundalini awakening is focusing on only one thing while meditating. If the mind is too active, it is impossible to experience a full awakening. Otherwise, it is too easy to be distracted or mesmerized by things around you, which can also happen in natural places. So to keep your mind focused on one thing makes kundalini awakening easier and more effective. Pick one specific thought or affirmation you want to memorize and repeat it to yourself while meditating. This will help reduce the stress and tension in your mind and keep you in a meditative state longer.

One common error is to regard spirituality or kundalini awakening as an end. You can avoid making this mistake by changing your perspective and how you talk about awakening. It is not a destination but a state of mind that you should strive for. This means anyone can experience it regardless of religion, age, or background.

Another thing is to stop asking when everything will get better during your first awakening. You can't measure it, and it depends on several factors. The awakening begins as you continue living a normal and healthy life. When and if this begins to happen depends on you, your environment, and your state of mind. You should not be too eager to know the answer, as it can cause stress. So keep yourself healthy and pay close attention to what happens around you. Once awakening begins, you will notice your feelings and conditions changing, which naturally means you start feeling better along the way. Do not deliberately or accidentally try to force a kundalini awakening because this will only cause an unpleasant situation that might shed light on the kundalini energy already awakened. The body is already preparing itself for the awakening process, and any further attempts can only cause damage.

If you go into awakening solely to gain psychic powers or even physical healing, your intentions are "impure", and your awakening may turn problematic. This does not mean you can't experience healing and miraculous powers during the awakening process; you can take advantage of them once awakened. But make sure you're aware of your intention and goal throughout so that you can avoid problems as you transform. This end goal contaminates your practice and impacts your health, chakras, and intellect.

Surround yourself with positive people or positive thoughts for the sake of uplifting your spirits. As you slowly progress into the awakening process, you must build a strong support system around you that you can rely on.

Avoid Power and Control Issues

Another issue often encountered by kundalini awakening beginners is the desire to gain power and control over others. This cannot be allowed to happen, and the true purpose of kundalini awakening is to do good and help others. The human ego and lust for power make this a common error. The awakening process is about helping yourself, regardless of what you do to others. So do not concern yourself with

If you are constantly looking outside yourself for answers, you are likely to become imbalanced during the awakening process. Look deep within yourself, and don't be afraid to confront aspects of yourself that you don't like. But you should also pick helpful self-development articles and avoid contradicting and useless ones.

Chances are, you won't see big changes in your behavior and actions once kundalini awakening begins. The time it takes to awaken fully varies from person to person, and the day's main focus is on your meditation and yoga sessions. This time may vary depending on your disposition and purpose in life. Be patient. The best way to wake up is to be fully aware of what happens around you.

Don't cling to the past or cling to anything or anyone. Give yourself time and space to heal. Do not rush to judgment or force anything; let the natural order do its job. Also, do not force kundalini awakening; otherwise, allow it to happen naturally. Do not hinder your growth by forcing things to happen; be patient with your mind and body and how they react throughout the awakening process.

Don't give up on yourself, even if you feel connected with something and experience something beyond your comprehension. Instead, be open to learning more and understand the nature of your existence. Don't commit errors along the way, such as trying to force something to happen or choosing the wrong spiritual practice.

Always do your research, and don't blindly follow others' practices. While there are similarities between practices, they are different and do not always have the same effects. Research what you're into and what works best for your body. Keep in mind that research does not mean blindly following a certain practice,

While your kundalini awakening practice is important, try not to become too attached to your routines, even if they are geared toward growth. If you are deprived of your practice, remember that spiritual development can occur without practice or routine. There is nothing wrong with a varied approach; you shouldn't stick to one practice for life.

While kundalini awakening is spiritual development, it does not mean you should be separated from others or detach yourself from your body. Instead, be more aware and composed within your mind and body boundaries. Remember that your consciousness is your true self and is separate from your body and mind. Kundalini awakening can help individuals feel freer than they have ever felt.

Chapter 8: Kundalini Expert Sessions

It is time to move on to the expert sessions as you have mastered Kundalini's awakening. I will go more in-depth into using mantras, pranayama or breathing practices, mudras or hand gestures, and some meditation.

You can now align your chakras and invite the serpent to rise after learning about the chakras and what they do. You will also receive the activation and learn how to activate it through a direct experience. You will be taught how to live harmoniously with Earth and its energies. You will also learn energy clearing and protection exercises.

Meditation for your Kundalini

Meditation unlocks the higher realms of consciousness and leads to enlightenment. In life, people have different experiences based on their individual beliefs, karma, and intuitive gifts. Psychics have unique experiences depending on the gifts given to them by the Divine and what they have learned through their journey and lifetime. Break through the barriers of illusion and past trauma and delve into your inner self with meditation's healing properties. Here are some meditation practices that you can use to awaken your Kundalini.

Enjoying Nature and Sounds

Basking in the Sun

- The first thing to do is to find a comfortable position outdoors, on the floor or in a chair, as the sun rises.

- Then, close your eyes and focus on the breath as you inhale and exhale.
- Imagine Kundalini rising along with the primordial sound Om as you inhale and let go of the sound as you exhale.
- Feeling the heat of the sun's rays as it shines on your body allows your spiritual energy to rise along with the serpent and merge with your higher self.
- Visualize an energy vortex and allow it to take you into higher consciousness.
- Finally, let go and visualize a beautiful white light coming out of the crown and dissolving the serpent. This practice is a form of active meditation.

Splashing in Waters

- Consider yourself alone on a beach or by a cool, clear lake.
- Allow yourself to breathe deeply for a few seconds and release tension in your shoulders and neck.
- Imagine a free-flowing wave of white light in your central channel, turning the water white around you. Become one with the sloshing of water and let your body absorb the light; the healing fills you completely.
- After a few minutes, return to the space where the white light flowed freely in your visualization and feel confident moving forward.

Walking on Water

- Feel your feet at the edge of the water you are sitting on or standing on, allowing it to kiss the tops of your feet. Consider the feelings of rootedness and fully awaken your Kundalini in a path where you feel the water on your journey to get in touch with yourself.

- Feel yourself being guided to that wave and surround your body as a wave of love.
- Feel the energy of the water activate your center and empower your being. Then, open your eyes and feel the energy flowing through your body from head to toe. Allow it to take you on the next step of your journey, envision yourself on the path of illumination, and be one with the Divine.

Joyful Chanting

- Spending time with your friends and loved ones with arms raised and strong voices is a fun way to share your joy. Simply expand your heart and feel the power of joy filling you to overflow.
- Sing a strong, resounding song to everyone around you and feel the sounds reverberating through your body.
- Ask your friends to raise their hands over their heads while singing, inviting them to the celebration of joy.
- Voices harmonized as one empowers the other to feel ecstatic, joyful, and open to the energetic vibrations from being around the other.
- Then imagine the cosmic serpent curled up in your spine, rising and spreading its energy throughout your body.

The Siren's Song

- Find a serene area near a body of water where you can find some quiet time or possibly dip into the water.
- As soon as you feel receptive, close your eyes and let your mind empty.
- Visualize the moving waters in front of you and feel the energy of the waves as you consume them. Imagine being in the primordial sea with the cosmic serpent curled up in your center as you float on the waters and breathe deeply.

- Visualize rising energy as you face the sky, and let the water rise with you. Visualize the sun shining in your eyes and feel alive and vibrant.
- Imagine the waves crashing against your crown chakra and feel inner peace as you open to allowing Kundalini to burst through. Know that the cosmic serpent opens you to higher consciousness and opens you up to some of the best times of your life.

Kundalini's Snake Dance

Dance is a dynamic expression that allows you to drop inhibitions and experience your primal self. Shamans, in ancient times, used dance to communicate with the spirit world. Dance allows you to let go and express your energetic being while moving your body to a wide series of rhythms and sounds.

- Start with a few warm-up movements. How you like to start is up to you. You can dance sensually and energetically or find your individual style that makes you feel free and which, empowers you, and makes you feel confident.
- Find music that makes you happy or that plays to your soul and allows you to let the energy move through you as you dance.
- Turn up the music and move in synchronicity to the rising energy.
- As the music continues playing, fill up with energy from the cosmic serpent as it rises and embraces your essence.
- Remember to breathe deeply and allow yourself to let go. Allow yourself to become one with the rising cosmic serpent and feel a joyous expression of your inner self.

Kundalini awakening causes people to become aware of higher planes of consciousness, and some even gain access to them. As a result, many people have felt psychic powers awakened along with the Kundalini energy, including clairvoyance and the ability to foretell the future.

Chakra Alignment

As you vibrate, you become open and receptive to the cosmic power and light that comes into your body through your crown chakra. Remember that there always is a way to overcome any fears or doubts that keep you from practicing meditation, breathing techniques, yoga, or any other exercise. Start by developing a daily practice, then build on it. As your Kundalini awakens, you will feel more positive emotions and be less stressed.

How to Align your Chakras

Aligning your Chakras can cleanse and balance your energy centers, creating positive energy flow throughout your being. There are guided processes that can help do this, and they can also help restore healthy balance to your being.

For the Root Chakra

- Align your root chakra by sitting comfortably on the floor, crossing your legs in Lotus position, or resting your feet on a chair with its back to a wall and at about 45 degrees to the floor.
- Close your eyes and focus on your breathing as your Kundalini rises in your center.
- Visualize yourself as a tree with deep roots that hold you strongly, drawing in nourishment from the earth. Your root chakra brings you feeling grounded and firmly planted.
- Close your eyes and imagine a strong, steady stream of light going from the center of your crown chakra straight

down the center of the spinal cord into the base of the spine. As you breathe deeply, try to imagine this light flowing across your body., illuminating and energizing the root chakra.

- Visualize light absorbed into your legs and feet and the bottoms of your feet bathed in white light.

For the Sacral Chakra

- Place your hands on your hips and your knees at your sides as you sit comfortably on the floor or a chair with a straight back and your feet flat on the floor.
- Close your eyes and imagine yourself as a young, energetic tree with branches sprouting from your hips.
- Feel the light and energy from the base of your spine move up to your hips and into the lower part of your chest, filling you with energetic vitality. This increases your energy and your physical strength, bringing a healthy balance of emotions to your being.
- Visualize this light swirling through your body as precious gold, illuminating and energizing the Sacral Chakra.
- Visualize the light absorbed into your legs, the lower part of your stomach, and your womb, energizing your feminine essence and nurturing your life force.

For the Solar Plexus Chakra

- Find a comfortable spot to sit or lie down.
- As you close your eyes, imagine a pillar of light from the start of your spinal column to the center of your abdomen, where it is absorbed in your solar plexus.
- Envision this light rushing through your body as precious gold, illuminating and energizing the solar plexus chakra. Visualize this light absorbed into your arms and your

solar plexus pool center, making you feel strong, confident, and energetic.

- When you were young, your buttocks were more rounded and firm than now. As you relax, feel the lightness and, at the same time, the strength of your buttocks, and you will feel a tingling sensation in your solar plexus.

For the Heart Chakra

- Find a comfortable place to take a seat or lay down.
- Close your eyes and imagine a pillar of light in the center of your body flowing out from the middle of your Spinal column to the center of the chest, where it is absorbed in your chest.
- Visualize this light flowing through your body, illuminating and energizing the heart chakra.
- Imagine the light as it is absorbed into your arms and through your heart area, creating warmth and love in a gentle flow that leads you to feel energized and wholesome in your heart.

For the Throat Chakra

- Find a comfortable spot to sit or lie down. Rest your back with your hands folded in your lap.
- Close your eyes and visualize a pillar of light radiating from the center of your spine to the center of your throat, where it is absorbed.
- Visualize the light as it is absorbed into your arms and through your throat, creating your ability to express yourself honestly and openly.

For the Third Eye Chakra

- Identify a comfortable place to sit or lie down.

- Consider a pillar of light in the center of your body, radiating upward between your brows from the base of your spinal column. Consider the light flowing through your body to your third eye chakra, illuminating and energizing it.
- Visualize the light as it is absorbed into your arms and through your eyebrows, creating the ability to see with clarity and inner vision. This light makes you aware of your consciousness of higher dimensions and other realities.

For the Crown Chakra

- Align your Crown Chakra by sitting comfortably on the floor or a chair with its back to a wall or in a lotus position. Rest your back with your hands folded in your lap.
- Imagine a pillar of light in the center of your body radiating from the center of your Spinal column to the very top of your head and slowly coming down spirally, showering your being with golden light and dissolving all blocks to your higher awareness.
- Focus on the golden light from all your chakras traveling down to the bottom of the spine and the root chakra while still keeping light streaming from your crown chakra to all parts of your being, cleansing and balancing all parts of you to achieve higher awareness.
- Sit for as long as you wish doing this practice, and slowly get up and open your eyes when you feel ready.

So here you can see how closely linked the Kundalini awakening is to physical freedom and spiritual awakening. The essence of Kundalini is that when the Kundalini awakens, it grows out of your root chakra and passes upward along the central channel, activating each chakra in turn. From the base of the spine, completely through the spine to the throat center, to the heart center, and so on to the crown center, the Kundalini energy is then directed down into the Earth; it then issues forth from the Earth traveling downward along the central channel emerging at the base of the spinal column again, making sure that all blockages are cleared, creating an uninterrupted flow of essential energy. Over time, by practicing these meditations daily, you start to experience an expansion in consciousness.

You must completely clear your mind to achieve a still and calm inner space. Keep this space in mind for as long as possible before proceeding to the next step. This powerful practice is used to help release blockages in the legs and the spinal column when starting a Kundalini energy flow. It involves getting into a comfortable position, then visualizing a golden snake climbing upward through the central channel of your body. As it passes through the central channels, it unblocks all the chakras and creates a deep connection between your lower and higher chakras. The inner attempt to stop the energy flow can be very strong, so do not struggle against it. You must practice this meditation for a good month to make progress. Allow this energy flow to happen naturally and incorporate it into your daily life.

When you feel imbalanced, call up your central channel and fill it with bright white light as you meditate. Imagine adding love to that light energy and carrying that vibration wherever you go. As you connect to the divine light inside of you, this light shines on the outside world and brightens everything. As you connect to the divine love inside you, that love amplifies and radiates outward. This is how you change the world. The light of the divine natural mind comes forth from within, and divine natural love and bliss come forth from within.

Starting on the spiritual path is a positive sign to the Universe that you are ready and open to expand and embrace your growing potential. Embracing the Kundalini energy means embracing an ever-growing connection and growth in consciousness, and the quest for expanding awareness and consciousness is never-ending. Kundalini will come out to play when the serpent is ready to rise. Count how many slow and steady cycles you can go through before being pushed into action.

After Kundalini Awakening

Upon awakening your Kundalini, accept and thank your body, and be proud of what it has accomplished for you. Kundalini is slow to fall asleep and may not settle down completely for weeks or months after awakening. A lot of expansion happens subconsciously, and you may sometimes feel overwhelmed or depressed.

It is normal to feel rattled; you may start crying or feeling odd sensations in your stomach. Listen only to yourself, not to others. When you feel negativity or unsafe feelings coming into your mind, this is a good time to use the three-minute technique to awaken your Kundalini. Once this technique is completed, you often realize that the negativity was nothing to be afraid of, and you can feel safe again. The desire to do good in the world may increase immensely, and you may have a strong desire to share whatever wisdom you become aware of with others. Synchronicity plays a crucial role in practicing Kundalini energy. Some people report a newfound sense of freedom after being introduced to this energy.

Kundalini is very common in many forms and expressions of yoga, and it is also present in many people who have practiced meditation and other spiritual practices for many years. It is never too late to awaken your own Kundalini energy. Children, the elderly, and people with severe mental limitations have experienced Kundalini energy during meditation or yoga. It is a part of everyone's makeup, and you are no exception. However, suppose you are not ready spiritually or physically, and you force the Kundalini up before it provides the natural opening. In that case, you may repeatedly experience these events for years to come until you overcome your fears and conditioning.

Be patient with yourself, and do not rush this process. You are embarking on the journey of a lifetime, one that will change your life forever and bring you closer to discovering what you are truly capable of accomplishing.

As you prepare to sleep, take a warm shower to stimulate your circulation and bring a refreshing glow to your skin. That night, listen to some beautiful music and visualize filling yourself with a crystal with white light energy, so you can use it as a healing tool in your sleep. Here are two other good exercises to help you sleep:

Know that your future interactions with your physical form will undoubtedly benefit your development. For one week before you attempt this exercise, commit not to engage in negative behaviors like smoking, drinking alcohol, etc. This allows the chakras to open more completely and absorb more energy.

You must have a reason for wanting to access higher planes of consciousness. To determine how to proceed, compare your goals to your higher self. After you are asleep, these realities change, and your higher self will communicate with you again. Allow your consciousness to drift into the universe as a star and into a state of pure awareness. When your mind wakes up again, it will be in a state of higher awareness.

Check in with your Kundalini to ensure it isn't overburdened or exhausted, and avoid pushing things to higher planes of consciousness. Observe your subtle energy bodies and observe your body's subtle reactions. Before you awaken your

Kundalini, you must clear the emotional blockages causing you to hold back. An emotional conflict like anger, resentment, or fear often blocks you from moving forward and must be dealt with before any spiritual progress is made. Whatever events happen in your life after your awakening of the Kundalini will also influence the growth of your spirituality, so remember to be grateful for everything you experience.

If you are having serious difficulties in your day-to-day life, you need to consider giving up the painful relationships and activities in your life that do not serve you. You can meditate to gain clarity and insight into what is happening and holding you back. You may also need emotional healing through counseling or therapy to balance your chakra energies.

Once you have awakened your Kundalini, it is important to stay grounded and centered, as this energy is constantly influencing you from within. It will manifest physically, such as twitches, shivers, or feelings of heat, as it moves through your body. Once you become used to it, this energy can manifest as a glowing sensation or an overwhelming amount of energy flowing through your body.

Allow Kundalini to guide you to your goals. Trust in this source energy vehicle and feel the presence of your angels and guardians. Listen to your body's wisdom and follow it.

Items to Use to Help Awaken Kundalini Energy

Crystals

Using crystals while meditating can also help awaken the Kundalini energy by transforming its color from dark to clear. Amethyst is a good choice for this purpose because it releases stress and promotes the release of natural endorphins into your body. The crystal's vibration can also help your chakras vibrate more harmoniously.

Generator crystals are crystals that are grounded at the base and hold energy for ease of use. They vibrate with the central frequency of the chakras and can help to raise Kundalini energy and help you clear chakras when you program them to clear specific chakras or organs. The best generator crystals are the 6-sided crystals such as the amazonite, sugilite, fluorite, and quartz crystals. Generator crystals are best to use first thing in the morning so your body can absorb their energy over several hours. One way to do this is to program them with your higher self before bedtime. Crystal wands work well as generator crystals because they can enhance where you want to go or what you want to do.

Crystals like lapis lazuli, blue lace agate, or green aventurine can help clear negative energies. Kyanite and carnelian crystals can be used to help you experience calm. Blue and clear quartz crystals can stimulate your chakras and reopen them if they are closed.

Singing Bowls

Singing bowls can bring your Kundalini energy to the surface safely. If you rung into a sacred space, they can clear your auric field of negativity and negative energy fields. They are most effective when you use them in combination with music or take place in a healing or ritual setting. A caring person who supports you whenever you raise your Kundalini can also help greatly. This energy comes from the divine natural mind and protects you from negative energies and attacks. Singing bowls can help you gently raise this energy or clear negative energy fields, and you can use these bowls in many different ways.

You can sing a mantra or "ohm" into the bowl as it vibrates. A sound bath is another great way to raise Kundalini energy. Play the singing bowl for 30 minutes, focusing on deep, cleansing breaths and opening your heart chakra as you sing. Sit or lay down with the bowl in front of you, focusing on keeping your hands and head still. Close your eyes and breathe fully and deeply. If you prefer, you can blend essential oils into the bowl to create an aromatherapy experience while you sing. If you are practicing yoga, you can run chanting through a singing bowl before and after you practice to create harmony in your yoga practice and gain deeper insight into the practice.

Practice Yoga

Yoga is the system that best encourages the awakening of the Kundalini energy. Not only can yoga teach you to relax and release stress with its many techniques, but it also stimulates your chakras and balances your energy fields. Yoga is a means of unifying your body, mind, and spirit. By practicing yoga regularly, you can learn how to connect with your chakras and the other subtle energy bodies within you that influence your physical experience. Kundalini energy is best awakened when you practice yoga daily for at least three months. Learning how to breathe while practicing yoga can help you learn to release the pent-up emotions and stress that are holding you back.

You can also learn to breathe deeply and consciously as you meditate to release positive and negative energies from your chakras and other areas of your life. Some of the yoga poses that you can perform to awaken your Kundalini energy are:

- Tadasana or mountain pose
- Bhujangasana or cobra pose
- Savasana or corpse pose
- Marichyasana or heron pose

Many postures can trigger your Kundalini when it is ready to awaken and stimulate the chakras. You can also call the Kundalini energy to you through mantras and use other techniques to become a conscious conductor of this energy.

You can take yoga classes to learn how to practice yoga safely, or you can practice yoga at home. Yoga is adaptable to your lifestyle, so no matter how busy you are, you can learn to incorporate it to feel more relaxed and balanced.

Music

- Music with specific frequencies can help your Kundalini awaken. The binaural beats in music are a powerful method for awakening higher levels of consciousness. They can be useful for those who have never awakened the Kundalini before because it creates a mild sense of nausea in the body that induces an altered state of consciousness. Another way music can stimulate the chakras is by playing the music on speakers while sitting and sitting in front of the speaker while lying on the floor. This facilitates syncing your mind with the upper chakras and helps bolster your resolve to move forward into higher planes of consciousness. Music can also help your chakras harmonize, especially if you listen to one piece of music while you meditate and another while you do yoga. Some classical music compositions are made under binaural frequencies.

Remember to raise the frequency of your voice as you do so so that it resonates more harmoniously with the lower and higher chakras. For example, slowly lowering and raising your voice naturally lowers your frequency because it breaks up the syllables and certain phonetics. You should keep connecting your mind to the higher frequency as you repeat the words. Sanskrit words are spiritually beneficial because they help us connect with the subconscious mind and access higher planes of consciousness.

Totem

If you want to access higher levels of consciousness, make sure you have a way to return to your original plane of consciousness. Bring something to remind you which world is real. A totem can help center you as you become overwhelmed by your Kundalini energy, reminding you of your origin and purpose. Because totems help you stay grounded and centered, it's generally a good idea to use a symbol that invokes a sense of love and connection. Some indigenous cultures believe the spiritual world is linked to the natural world. This is why animals are often used to represent gods or spirits. Invoking animal totems to get you to higher planes can introduce powerful forces into your life. Don't be surprised when a totem appears to you, even if you don't have a close connection to animals or the natural world. They may have been sent to you to help you understand a facet of yourself.

An animal totem can help you understand your spiritual evolution. Certain animals can help you awaken your full potential to fulfill your destiny or spiritual calling. Once you awaken the Kundalini, it gives you access to spiritual mechanisms that help you manifest your dreams and goals. Still, don't let it control you.

Animals most commonly signify the Kundalini represented love and divinity, such as owls, cats, eagles, snakes, dolphins, and wolves. Some animals are more connected to spiritual powers, such as soul groups, and can represent entirely different spiritual entities. The animal that is attracted to you depends on your spiritual quest and your spiritual development. These animals can evoke numerous spiritual entities, so keep your connection to the animal strong, and you won't be harmed as you evolve. It is important to note that many of these animals have a dark side, and the animal's power increases with the darkness within you.

The Kundalini energy can be overwhelming initially, but that means you are close to succeeding on your spiritual path. Don't rush yourself. Instead, let yourself experience all of the good this energy can bring to your life. Once you overcome the initial resistance and awaken the Kundalini energy, you will feel like you have a new lease on life. This personal calling inspires you and helps you evolve as a person. You will no longer need to run from life or hide from life.

Chapter 9: Projection of Psychic Gifts

Kundalini assists people in traveling to higher planes of consciousness and achieving psychic gifts. As your Kundalini awakens, you start developing or reawakening abilities that can enable you to do dormant things. But we need to look closely at what that means.

For generations, people have been taught about harnessing their power to get ahead in life and make money. This is the top-down system we live in, and it has been around ever since we got off the boat and started building societies on the seashore and in woodlands.

However, many people are now starting to question this belief system because they are forced to work so hard to get back so little. This is reminiscent of what artists experienced in the Middle Ages when painters did the artwork for the church in exchange for food and shelter. This killed the creativity of artists because doing art was secondary to survival.

Society has suppressed awakened souls for eons, and now is the time for people to rise up and reclaim their souls. The elite few have worked hard to convince people that we are machines that don't make smart choices every day of our lives. But the truth is exactly the opposite. We are infinitely intelligent beings capable of changing the world with the power of the mind. This is what awakening Kundalini is all about.

The descent of Kundalini is the descent into your soul. We are taught from a young age to disregard our souls and forget who we are. That's why we don't use the intelligence of the soul to create lives the way we should. Instead, we create our lives based on what others think we should be like. The soul wants to ascend into its Higher Self and do great things, but the mind keeps putting it down. Instead, it wants us to march into the rat race every week and slave away for low pay and low-quality food. The mind takes us away from the higher planes of consciousness and puts us in the lowest energy frequency possible, making us feel trapped and suffering throughout the majority of our lives.

As you open yourself to your spiritual power, you can develop intuition and psychic abilities. But be aware that tools such as tarot cards and other things of energy like this are only useful to a point, and you need your connection and connection to your Higher Self to use these tools effectively.

Kundalini is energy, just like electricity is energy. If you tap into your inner energy system, you can access your other gifts to channel energy into your body. Our nervous systems can maintain associative memory patterns because they learn through repetition, but we need to input new patterns. The mind needs us to develop our intuition and channel our energy into our bodies to rewire itself and become a new mind pattern that serves us rather than works against us.

Astral Projection

Astral travel is a person's conscious travel to another dimension using a body-mind connection. We are all capable of astral projecting because our thinking patterns have astral memories that uniquely influence our experiences.

Your everyday world and your astral world interconnect. You travel through your etheric body into your astral body in the dimension above your body and then project your astral body into another dimension to travel through different time zones. One of the reasons people want to astral travel is because they want a break from their reality to experience something epic. But many problems come with the practice, and it's recommended that you practice astral projection under the supervision of an expert until you know what you are doing.

People astral project in different ways. Some people simply travel to different time zones and experience things from other dimensions when awake, while others astral project while sleeping. Our minds can dream while we are awake and dream while we are asleep, but a lot of what is learned or experienced is blocked by what is known as the third eye.

We have an etheric body, an astral body, and a physical body, all connected by a root of energy known as the Kundalini. Our bodies need to work together effectively for us to control our dreams, and it's through our physical bodies that we learn how to control our dreams and then learn how to control them in astral spaces.

Astral travel can be used by practicing yogis and yoginis to expand their awareness to other dimensions. They do this by learning how to douse their physical body in a photon field that expands their mind to other vehicles of consciousness while maintaining their physical bodies.

When people first start practicing astral projection, they will likely have frightening experiences. But scares and bad dreams are a good way to open our hearts to new possibilities in a transformational way. It's important to keep in mind what astral projection involves. We are spirits in a human body with a web of connections to the Earth, the cosmos, and other minds from other dimensions. People can learn to feel safe after a time and start exploring things leisurely with the knowledge that they are back home when they wake up.

Astral travel is when a person consciously leaves their body and travels through dimensions and other universes, like in the movies or on television. Both good and evil beings use astral travel; those who have become adept practitioners of astral projection, such as the angels, can learn to access other dimensional planes and traverse the universes. People can also use astral projection to project their consciousness to other bodies and control bodies that belong to others while projecting their consciousness.

When people astral project, they travel through dimensions with a body-mind connection called the Kundalini. They leave behind their physical body, but their mind remains connected to their physical body. They are similar to a soul that has left the human body to travel. They often leave behind the vessel and find they can connect their physical body to the vehicle of consciousness they have left behind.

Moving into the Astral Plane

Clear your mind of all thoughts and emotions and any urges, desires, needs, or calculations. Maintain a peaceful, serene silence in your mind. Attend to the silence with compassion until you sense yourself as the mind and the body. Once you have a mind-to-body link or a connection, you can begin anchoring into the ethereal plane. Maintain your anchor by maintaining a state of stillness and peaceful silence and stillness. Your conscious attention will anchor you to the ethereal plane until you slow your breathing, and you can fully anchor to the ethereal plane. Then travel to the ethereal plane and practice traveling around the holographic universe clockwise and then counterclockwise.

Allow kundalini to flow through your chakras, activating the central channel as it rises and falls. Visualize yourself flying in an expanding white light as it fills your entire body before ascending into consciousness. Now that you are connected with your higher self, you can travel to the ethereal plane for 1-2 hours, practice traveling, and return to your physical body. Repeat for 3-4 consecutive days, then travel to the astral plane and try to traverse the sky from within your body. When traveling within the astral plane, stabilize your energy and connect with your higher self and your angelic guides and protectors. Practice traveling the astral plane until you are completely safe and then journey to the crystalline city.

Before embarking on the cosmic journey, you should partially ground yourself by understanding that your mind has more power than your body. To do this, imagine a different body and start moving each finger and toe separately. Connect your subtle energy layer to the astral project as you slowly gain mobility. As your astral body separates from your physical body, you should feel a buzzing at the edge of your being. You will feel different sensations as you ascend from the physical realm to the non-physical realm. Your soul floats above your body, exploring your room and house before venturing outside. You will often experience the strong feeling that something or someone is there when no one seems to be there. Your consciousness is in a higher realm known as a semi-trance state. You may experience visions and sounds as you do this type of exploration.

Astral travel occurs as the mind detaches from the physical senses and becomes completely immersed in the dreamscape. Your dreams become surreal as your senses slowly detach from your physical body. You get disoriented and unsure of your surroundings and objects as you lose your sense of touch, lock, taste, sight, hearing, and smell. Your mind starts to understand that you are dreaming and conscious of the separation. You will float through light clouds, feel the colors around you, and see what is beyond the physical realm. You can look into mirrors and experience other-selves and faces.

The root cord is the physical and energetic link between your astral and physical bodies. Remember to keep this cord in mind as you explore your room or home. Never wander too far from your root cord, as you need to return to it. You will sometimes hear a voice knocking at the door or someone calling your name when you wake up. If you experience this, follow the sound of that person's voice back to your room and your root cord so that you are safely guided back to your physical self when you wake up.

When you open your consciousness to other worlds and dimensions, practice healing your fear of the unknown and being afraid. Experience your limits and your inner strength. Understand that you are more than your physical body and experience sensations and feelings that transcend your physical body to draw on your inner strength. Allow yourself to explore the astral plane you've discovered, but stay on the earth plane first to avoid becoming overwhelmed.

As you explore the astral realm, you'll see the attar of a blue lotus floating in the sky and see millions of spirits moving through it. Feel the wind on your skin and hear crystals tinkling as you ascend to the astral realm. Then you will see a starry sky filled with countless stars and start to travel through it. You can travel and explore different dimensions by shifting your focus to different illusions of light.

Other Psychic Gifts and Clairvoyance

If you want to experience a good level of psychic awakening, awakening your Kundalini will allow you to access more psychic abilities. One benefit of this journey is knowing that you have a purpose and are more than your physical being. You can explore the unknown from a higher perspective. You'll learn to let go of fear and relax your energetic centers as you open your consciousness to a greater level of understanding.

Aura Reading

Aura reading is a psychic gift that everyone has their interpretation of, so don't be concerned if yours differs from others. The core meaning of aura reading is understanding, observing, and interpreting a person's aura. Your aura is the energy surrounding you. As a human, you're made up of energy particles called electrons and protons. These energies interact in different energetic patterns, and you'll better understand these patterns if you can read them. The makeup of your aura reflects your spiritual nature, which is why it can offer deep insight into a person's character, abilities, and intentions. When you've practiced reading auras, you'll find that some people are easy to read, but others are not. When a person's mind is strong, and at peace, their perspective will be much clearer.

Aura reading involves understanding the energetic color patterns and how they change when a person makes an emotional adjustment or changes their state of being. For example, pink is a calming color, and the color of pink in the aura will change if a person is feeling anything other than peace. Be patient when you're learning to read auras; you will find it easier to connect and understand each color pattern as you learn to interpret different energetic patterns in other people's auras. Even if the person you're reading has a dark or murky aura, you can use it as a baseline to connect and understand others.

Soul Channeling

Channeling is an ability that allows a person to allow another spirit to speak through them temporarily. A vessel is someone another spirit has chosen to give messages through. Spiritual channels can channel angels, archangels, guides, ancestors, ascended masters, or past life experiences. A person channeling may temporarily allow a spirit to take over their body and voice if quaking in fear. However, a person with a stronger mind can pass transcend fear and allow the spirit to speak through them.

A spirit's message may seem as though it's coming from inside a person's mind, but your spirit guides will hear the vibration of the message. As you focus on the spirit's message, your spirit guides will translate for you. The spirit that becomes a part of your awareness will communicate through you. It will offer its message and then leave. You don't always need to hear a message to be affected by it physically. Sometimes a spirit will connect with your higher mind so that you're carried along on a wave of light energy as you receive a message meant to reach your soul. Many people aren't even aware that they are channeling their messages.

Clairgustance

Clairgustance is a psychic ability that allows people to taste something before putting it on their tongue. It's similar to tasting someone's energy before touching them. However, it's spiritual wisdom and knowledge instead of physical taste. A clairgustance person may also have a vivid dream before tasting.

Awakening your Kundalini energy can bestow you the power of clairgustance, and you'll notice that you can taste a person's spirit before they talk to you or spend time around you. You may not always receive clear messages or perceive them clearly as you receive them. When your mind is open, your spirit guides will give you the necessary information. You can meditate to receive messages. Your spirit guides will communicate with you differently, and you'll sometimes feel their presence. People can also communicate with you as an alien would communicate with them.

Clairalience

Clairalience is the ability to smell things not normally smelled by humans. This ability is not very common and can sometimes be difficult to hone. A person with clairalience may catch a faint scent when others don't smell anything and may feel unsure about what it's trying to tell them. They may find themselves smelling things they can't pinpoint or fully understand. Some people may be sensitive to other people's energy and cologne or perfume, which can cause them to be oversensitive to odors and perception.

Clairalience is connected to another psychic gift called omniscentism. Omniscentism is the ability to see and smell the world in infinite detail and is a gift that some people don't believe exists. If you feel that you have this psychic gift, don't ignore it. You can develop your psychic abilities further and enjoy using your gift daily if you choose to develop it.

Clairalumination

Clairalumination is the ability to see spirits using a white ray of light. The light passes through your eyes, and you can feel it enter your body. Clairalumination is used for mediumship to help people see what's happening in the spirit world. Clairalumination is also used by spirit guides to help them see what's going on in the physical world.

Some more awakened and aware people can speak with their spirit guides in meditation or out-of-body experiences. You have a spirit guide who watches and guides you on your soul journey. The soul journey is your soul's purpose in this physical world. Your spirit guide will support you on your path and help you learn through life lessons you experience along the way. A spirit guide doesn't speak directly with us all the time; they're busy working in the spirit world and helping us learn what needs to be learned.

Clairaudience

Clairaudience is similar to clairsentience, but it's a psychic hearing ability. Some clairaudient people can hear words without translating them into meaning. They just hear voices in their mind somewhere that they can't pinpoint. These voices may be angels, guides, or family members who have passed. The voices may warn of upcoming events or describe things you can't put into words.

You can achieve hearing beings in another realm by awakening your Kundalini. Clairaudient people can tap into their higher mind and sense the universe's vibrations. Your subconscious mind is connected with your higher consciousness. You can ask your higher mind to help you tap into the ability by exposing you to voices and sound waves. Make an effort to listen to voices outside your mind when you're outside. You'll notice that it's not always the voice that matters; it is the intention behind it. If a voice speaks to you with a harmful message, the negative vibration will destroy your frequency, and your illusion will be shattered. Negative voices aren't always bad; if you hear voices trying to tell you good friends are in trouble, for example, it's a good idea to go and help them.

Clairsentience

Clairsentience is a psychic ability that lets people feel events before they happen. It's similar to getting a gut feeling that something is going to happen or that someone is thinking about you before they do. Clairsentience can be very subtle, uncomfortable feelings of uneasiness that are hard to understand unless you have the same feelings. This ability can warn of incoming dangers or present choices you may not want to make.

Clairsentience is the ability to feel another person's pain or concerns, and many people with this gift discover their gift in their teens. Clairsentience is linked with empathy, sympathy, compassion, social skills, relationships, and intuition. People with strong clairsentience listen to their bodies and what they tell them. People who learn to hone their clairsentience gifts become very in tune with others.

Clairvoyance

You can achieve clairvoyance once your Kundalini is awakened. Thousands of people would seek out psychics who claim to have this ability daily, but true clairvoyants are rare. If you're open-minded, have moderate anxiety without being too anxious, and can turn off your emotions, you may develop clairvoyant abilities. Your mind needs to be completely still and quiet. If you meditate and tolerate quiet time alone in your subconscious mind for 15 to 20 minutes daily, you'll increase your chances of becoming clairvoyant. The heightened energy allows you to observe life in the spirit world and become more in touch with your higher conscience.

Clairvoyant souls awakened by Kundalini energy can perceive an event or look for signs of an event in the physical world that occurs in the spirit world. The clairvoyant is a human with two personalities and can simultaneously see all things earthly and heavenly. Clairvoyant people receive messages about loved ones already in the spirit world. They receive messages about scientists who solve problems or create new projects and messages from a universe composed of energy.

Divination

Divination has been long practiced by awakened souls who have received messages of guidance from the spiritual world. Some messages come in dreams. Others come from visions, and some people receive messages randomly. Every person has a different method of divination, but each method is the same. Divination is the use of messages that open consciousness to greater understanding. The messages may come in many forms and from many sources, including spirit guides, angels, or the Higher Self.

Divination can take the form of art and photography, dance, music, games, simple daydreaming, tuning forks and chimes, and other forms of expression from meditation and drills. A form of divination that can be helpful for some people is developing a dream journal. For example, if you want to become clairvoyant, make an effort to write down your dreams when you go to bed. Your dream journal will be your friend's, so record everything with details you can remember when you wake up. Some people think dreams are meaningless random nonsense, but many have messages that are only revealed upon awakening. If you're in a dream and don't consciously choose to remember it, you may wake up feeling agitated or confused at the message you didn't understand. Everything that exists has a vibration, including human beings. When you get messages similar to anxiety, it proves that anxiety comes from the spirit world, not your worries.

Dowsing

Dowsing is achieved when a group communicates with spirits by using pendulums. Dowsing is done using simple pendulums, or one may set up a dowsing rod to include multiple pendulums in the dowsing rod and draw dowsing rods in sand or water. The dowsing rod or pendulum is placed over a specific area or object to seek spiritual guidance. Once the pendulum or dowsing rod bobs over one area or object, the group may interpret the information they're receiving about their location or object in front of you.

Empathic Abilities

Empathy is the ability to sense a person's feelings and emotions, even if that person is far away. Some empaths may feel like someone's energy is draining away after only being near them for a few minutes. People who are empaths can often feel emotions radiating from others and feel they're being taken advantage of by certain situations or people. However, empaths know this is due to past traumatic events they've had to experience. They can sense, absorb, and process other people's emotions while feeling them. This helps them heal as they can release those emotions by feeling them first.

Heightened Intuition

Intuition is an underappreciated psychic gift, and mediumship is a highly sought-after psychic ability for communicating with those who have died. Kundalini awakening can assist you in developing your psychic abilities, but be careful what you wish for. As your psychic abilities improve, you may struggle as you're constantly bombarded with messages lacking complete clarity and truth. Your heightened intuition may also cause fear as you realize that not everyone has good intentions and that you can easily be deceived. Your intuition can become disrupted by exposure to negative energies through stressful work situations or human interactions.

Mediumship

Spiritual awakenings can trigger our bodies to become sensitive to souls in another realm, to which they act as mediums.

Mediumship allows a spirit to pass messages from the spirit world to the physical world. A medium can communicate with spirits, angels, guides, and past lives. Mediumship is the ability to see, hear, feel, and see spirits. This practice is the art of communication between dimensions. A good medium has a strong mind and body that can exert control when facing circumstances that could lead to fear, which could cause the spirit to shut him out and prevent him from channeling.

Past Life Regression

Remembering your past lives can happen as you awaken your Kundalini. Experiencing your past lives can teach you a lot about life. If you're already awakening your Kundalini, you may experience some of your past life memories during meditation. As you travel to your past lives during past-life regression, you may relive a part of your life. You may be a shop owner, know how to help others through their difficult times, and may remember having children or meeting someone who shares memories with you. You may see and feel moving through life the same way you did then.

During your Kundalini awakening, you can consciously start being able to visualize events that are happening far away in the physical world. Your mind becomes filled with pure energy, allowing messages from the spirit world to manifest and be interpreted through visualization instead of your ears and audio equipment. Once you learn to open your mind to the spirit world and receive messages through meditation, you can access information from everywhere and see places you have never been.

Psychic Protection

You may feel confused, intimidated, and panicked when under a psychic attack. Some psychic attacks are very subtle and are meant to manipulate your state of mind and beliefs. Once you're attacked and performed under psychic attack, you may feel more depressed and afraid of experiencing another psychic attack in the future. Anyone who's experienced paranormal events for an extended period is now regularly subject to psychic attacks. Psychic attacks are triggered by putting more effort into pursuing your dreams, becoming more in tune with your intuition, and becoming more sensitive to energy emanations and vibrations.

Precognition

The psychic ability to see into the future is known as a premonition. A person with a premonition may see images or interpret physical sensations as they happen. A premonition may warn you of an upcoming event so you can take the necessary precautions to prevent it. However, a premonition can also be a negative event in the future. Since your mind may interpret what you wish to happen as a premonition rather than reality, this may lead to a negative premonition. Someone with a negative premonition might worry about an upcoming negative event happening to them when they could potentially avoid that event altogether if they changed how they thought about it.

Awakened people can use their Kundalini energy to see the future, but only if they want it to happen. If your destiny is set in stone, you can never change it, no matter how hard you try. Use premonitions to determine your next move, but don't do it as an excuse to wag your finger at others and point at your future negative events.

Receiving Messages from Angels and Spirit Guides

Guardian angels and spirit guides are spiritual beings sent to guide and protect living beings on Earth. Guardian angels are assigned to a particular individual, while spirit guides are assigned to a particular family unit or tribe. Guardian angels and spirit guides sometimes appear human-like figures with glowing or transparent wings. Angels, ancestors, and spirit guides can also help you during certain life transitions, such as getting married or starting a new job. You may feel like you're talking to yourself when you make a comment you don't want to make, question something you shouldn't question, or say something out of character to a family member or friend. Guardian angels and spirit guides can send you images or messages to help you stay focused on what life path you're meant to take.

Retrocognition

Retrocognition is seeing back in time in your mind's eye. Sometimes it's as if you're looking through a camera to capture a moment in time. Retrocognition allows you to see events as they happened, but this does not mean you have these memories and events documented in your memory. Retrocognition allows you to recall past events to stay in touch with the people you once knew worldwide or remember the family members and friends who have died.

Telepathy

Telepathy is the ability to mentally communicate through images and sounds without using words. Telepathy usually requires a quiet mind and clear thinking. Someone who's highly imaginative with an appropriate amount of anxiety may have the anxiety required to become telepathic. However, a hectic and stressful lifestyle will diminish your telepathic abilities. Those who can control their emotions and stay calm under stress are more attuned to telepathy.

Final Thoughts

Kundalini Awakening can let you see your dreams and reality through a spiritual lens. Psionic abilities can make you more vulnerable to energy changes and vibrations. Reactive programming against psychic abilities may keep you from believing in your abilities and opening your mind to the spirit world. Opening your mind can be a positive experience if you're ready to develop latent psychic abilities and increase your psionic abilities. Psychic abilities can also protect you against psychic attacks. With the help of your spirit guides, angels, and guardian spirits, you may be able to grow stronger in your spiritual energy, experientially feel past lives, see your future, and communicate with supernatural beings. Understanding psionics and learning to create your reality can be useful for healing and spiritual growth. Information provided is general in nature and cannot serve as a replacement for individual medical, emotional, or spiritual support and guidance.

These physical and intellectual changes can cause you to be more sensitive. You'll need to practice good habits to help balance your sensitivities, so you don't lose your mind. Your Kundalini is your spiritual energy, and it's awakened during your spiritual awakening. Once you awaken your Kundalini, you can use it as a psychic shield to protect you against psychic attacks, access your higher self, increase your clairvoyant and empathetic abilities, feel your Higher Self throughout life, meditate while healing, and more.

The energy your Kundalini awakens is the sacred spiritual energy that can help you see the past, speak the languages of your spiritual ancestors, communicate with spirit and guides, see the future, and more. Since you're already aware of spirituality and practice meditation, psionics is most likely something you already know deep down inside. You must understand that awakening your Kundalini energy can open your higher chakras and allow negative energy to enter your being, causing pain and discomfort. Be aware that negative spirits or energy may be trying to block you from awakening your Kundalini energy. Your body and mind may be alert to heat, cold, tingling, pressure, and pulsating sensations. These sensations are expected and normal, but they may become so intense that they can be unbearable. You'll also feel sensations running throughout your body. Your energy is high, which may cause you to feel more alert, energetic, passionate, and creative. You may be more attracted to energy or people or feel physically touched even without romantic touching.

Psychic abilities are abilities that display a variety of paranormal powers, such as telepathy, clairvoyance, and telekinesis. They are often referred to as supernatural or occult powers. Psionics is the study of psychic abilities and space-time manipulation. Since psionics requires the power of concentration, psychics are more in tune with their psychic abilities than others and can manipulate them more subconsciously than others. However, you can develop psychic abilities throughout life. Maybe you're experiencing intrusive thoughts and exteriorizing your anxieties. Maybe your anxiety is causing you to feel unsafe and vulnerable right now. Maybe your anxiety has earned you a reputation in the medical community as an anxious person, but you don't believe you are anxious and are waiting for someone to prove you wrong.

Kundalini awakening and psychic abilities can help you grow spiritually and overcome your trauma from post-traumatic stress disorder. However, if your PTSD is severe, you'll suffer from anxiety attacks, and these panic attacks can make you more prone to heightened anxiety and trauma. Free yourself from your past and anxiety with the help of angels, spirit guides, and your Higher Self. When your Kundalini awakens, you experience out-of-body journeys, visions of your Higher Self, experiences during dreaming, and more. You have the spiritual journey to heal your past trauma and grow spiritually. However, your anxiety keeps you from seeing your Higher Self and reaching enlightenment.

Your intuition is always trying to relay important information to you. You should be aware of what's happening around you, both in your everyday life and the world around you, so you can stay one step ahead of the situations you encounter. Develop a sixth sense and connect to the spirit world to better communicate with your intuition or guardian angels. If you're a psychic, you're also more susceptible to psionic attacks. These attacks attempt to control your emotions and behavior. As your Kundalini activates, you can develop clairvoyant abilities and see your subconscious thoughts telepathically. Although these abilities can help you develop stronger psychic powers and heal your psychic scars, they can also open you up to psychic attacks while you sleep. If you've been struggling with anxiety lately and are plagued with intrusive thoughts that don't make sense, there is a possibility that you're experiencing trauma.

Your higher consciousness, or Higher Self, is connected with the realm of angels and spirit guides, and if you can connect with your spirit guides and angels, they can help protect you from spiritual attacks. High levels of anxiety can affect your sleep and cause you to have poor sleep hygiene. If you've been experiencing high anxiety and trauma caused by your intrusive thoughts lately, it's a sign that your energy is very high. The anxiety you are experiencing is a sign that your Kundalini energy is awakening. You may also feel sensitive to other people and their moods. You may be able to feel other emotional vibrations, too. Because your energy is high, it may cause you to feel emotional and become even more emotionally unstable. You may feel extra conscious of your physical self because your energies are higher than ever before and more sensitive.

Practice healthy habits in remaining calm yet motivated, finding balance in remaining grounded and in control while connected to the energy you're channeling. Your Higher Self is the most powerful psychic ability that can help you feel your inner voice, your Higher Self's wisdom, and manage your psychic abilities, among other things. Your Higher Self is connected to the spirit world, translated into non-physical form. However, your Higher Self is related to you spiritually right now, and your guides or guardian spirits exist as spiritual entities in your mind and spirit form. They can teach you to meditate and heal through energy. Your Higher Self is best described as a mystical, spiritual entity in your spirit form that exists beyond time and space and knows everything that has happened throughout your life. Your Higher Self is spiritually connected to you through faith and trust, even if you don't believe in your psychic abilities and haven't accepted that your Higher Self exists. Having awakened your Kundalini may enable you to predict and prepare for future life events. Enjoy your newly-awakened Kundalini energy.

59 Positive Affirmations for Awakening your Kundalini

Positive affirmations express the belief that a certain thing is possible. They can benefit anyone striving for a goal by teaching them to think positively. Some people read positive affirmations every day to achieve specific goals. You can benefit by repeating these simple statements to yourself to help you overcome negativity and succeed at your goals.

Repeating positive affirmations help you reach any goal you strive for by increasing your self-confidence, building a positive attitude, and boosting your determination. This helps you visualize your goal and realize the importance of reaching it. This can be any goal you have on your mind!

Affirmations can help you reach your goals faster as they are positive thinking. They involve repeating a phrase or statement until it becomes "second nature."

Now relax and calm down as you repeat each affirmation five times in a row for 2 minutes each. You will listen to the affirmation, and there will be a pause of 2 minutes after each affirmation to give you enough time to repeat the affirmation and let your brain process it.

59 Affirmations for Awakening your Kundalini

1. I honor the Divine Spark that is within all beings.
2. My Divine Subconscious knows what is best for me.
3. My true destiny is to be happy and fulfilled.
4. I live life in Peace, Love, Harmony & Light.
5. I allow sacred vibrations to be self-evident in all things that I do.
6. I desire all good things for my highest good.
7. The loving energies of Mother Earth always surround me.
8. I am a Divine Being, experiencing life on earth in a physical and human body.
9. I attract to myself only what I desire.
10. I cleanse my mind of all negative thoughts.
11. I focus my energy on positive thoughts to raise my vibration and help me to attract more positive energy into my life.
12. My soul seeks to be awakened.
13. I open my heart to all that is good in humanity.
14. I calm my mind, body, and spirit through meditation and deep spiritual connection.
15. My thoughts are positive, uplifting, and healing.
16. I am a Divine Being having a human experience.
17. I am the Light of the world.
18. My purpose is to share love, give spiritual guidance and be a light for humanity.
19. All my needs are met easily and in perfect divine timing.
20. I stay positive, happy, and healthy in all areas of my life.
21. I accept the angels, guides, and ascended masters as personal guides in my life.
22. My mind is calm, peaceful, and focused.

23. I choose to feel inspired and open to creative thoughts and inspiration.
24. I let peace and tranquility rule my life.
25. I live harmoniously with myself, my community of family, friends, co-workers, and neighbors.
26. I am kind and courteous to all others.
27. I live in harmony with nature.
28. I am a member of the Divine Intelligence.
29. This vibration is within me and around me at all times.
30. My Higher Self is my storehouse of knowledge, understanding, and insight.
31. My Higher Power is delighted with me and always shares its abundance.
32. I sincerely desire to learn more about the spiritual journey and ascension process I embark on.
33. I desire to connect to my inner Divine Self.
34. I want to become healthier inwardly and outwardly.
35. I aim to find my Spiritual Path.
36. I live in harmony with all living things of the Universe.
37. There is a higher power with more to offer me than I can imagine.
38. I trust that the Universe loves me unconditionally.
39. I live a life aligned with my soul's highest good, Divine Plan, and purpose.
40. I want to continue your spiritual journey in a positive state of mind.
41. I am powerful, wonderful, and valuable.
42. I deserve happiness and joy in my life.
43. I deserve to speak my truth and share my gifts, talents, and abilities with the world.
44. My life is an amazing journey to create in any way you choose.
45. My life is an amazing journey to learn as much as I choose to learn and experience all that I can experience.

46. My life is a remarkable opportunity for all that I choose it to be.
47. I enjoy the journey of life I am living at this moment.
48. I choose to feel healthy, happy, and abundant in all areas of my life.
49. I lovingly release anything that no longer serves my higher good or the highest good of all living things and the Universe.
50. I forgive everything that no longer serves my Highest Good and the highest good of all living things and the Universe.
51. I forgive anyone who has harmed me or acted against me.
52. I forgive myself for past hurts and wounds that I hold inside.
53. I am destined to continue on my spiritual journey to enlightenment.
54. I evolve and blossom and rise to an even higher level.
55. I take steps to learn and expand my consciousness and awareness.
56. I call on divine help and guidance to assist me in all my endeavors.
57. I accept all beings as messengers from the Divine and a member of my higher family of Light.
58. I accept all the support and help I need to learn and grow as I simultaneously help others to do the same.
59. I completely believe that important information has the potential to help open many hearts and souls and to help erase the darkness.

MELISSA
GOMES

FREEBIES

AND

RELATED PRODUCTS

WORKBOOKS
AUDIOBOOKS
FREE BOOKS
REVIEW COPIES

HERE

HTTPS://SMARTPA.GE/MELISSAGOMES

Freebies!

I have a **special treat for you**! You can access exclusive bonuses I created specifically for my readers at the following link! The link will redirect you to a webpage containing all my books and bonuses for each book. Just select the book you have purchased and check the bonuses!

>> https://smartpa.ge/MelissaGomes<<

OR scan the QR Code with your phone's camera

Bonus 1: Free Workbook - Value 12.95$

This **workbook** will guide you with **specific questions** and give you all the space you need to write down the answers. Taking time for **self-reflection** is extremely valuable, especially when looking to develop new skills and **learn** new concepts. I highly suggest you *grab this complimentary workbook for yourself*, as it will help you gain clarity on your goals. Some authors like to sell the workbook, but I think giving it away for free is the perfect way to say **"thank you" to my readers**.

Bonus 2: Free Book - Value 12.95$

Grab a **free short book** with **22+ Techniques for Meditation**. The book will introduce you to a range of meditation practices you can use to help you develop your inner awareness, inner calm, and overall sense of well-being. You will also learn how to begin a meditation practice that works for you regardless of your schedule. These meditation techniques work for everyone, regardless of age or fitness level. Check it out at the link below!

Bonus 3: Free audiobook - Value 14.95$

If you love listening to audiobooks on the go or would enjoy a narration as you read along, I have great news for you. You can download the audiobook version of *my books* for **FREE** just by signing up for a FREE 30-day Audible trial! You can find the audio versions of my books (depending on availability) at the following link.

Join my Review Team!

Are you an avid reader looking to have more insights into spirituality? Do you want to get free books in exchange for an honest review? You can do so by joining my Review Team! You will get priority access to my books before they are released. You only need to follow me on Booksprout, and you will get notified every time a new Review Copy is available for my latest release!

For all the Freebies, visit the following link:

>> https://smartpa.ge/MelissaGomes<<

OR scan the QR Code with your phone's camera

I'm here because of you

When you're supporting an independent author,
you're supporting a dream. Please leave
an honest review on Amazon by scanning
the QR code below and clicking on the "Leave
an Amazon Review" Button.

https://smartpa.ge/MelissaGomes

Printed in Great Britain
by Amazon